Brooklyn Crazy Guy

Michael Castello

Order this book online at www.trafford.com
or email orders@trafford.com

Most Trafford titles are also available at major online book retailers.

Printed in the United States of America.

ISBN: 978-1-4669-1166-6 (sc)
ISBN: 978-1-4669-1168-0 (hc)
ISBN: 978-1-4669-1167-3 (e)

Library of Congress Control Number: 2012900615

Trafford rev. 04/24/2012

 PUBLISHING® www.trafford.com

North America & international
toll-free: 1 888 232 4444 (USA & Canada)
phone: 250 383 6864 ♦ fax: 812 355 4082

The Atlantic waters flowed through the ditches and into the heart of East New York. Homes were built on stilts that rose high above the marsh grasses. The construction of catwalks led to canals that were waterways to dry land. The cabana-type homes were painted white and had open balconies. At first they were occupied for summer use, but the Depression forced people to live in the cabanas. The winters were severe; the cabanas had no insulation, water, or electricity. Kerosene was the main source of heat; many house fires were started because of this, and men were burned to death. Others cleared land and made open pits to burn wood to keep warm. The homes were built with debris.

My dad would take me to the marshes to visit his friends. Many lived alone, waiting for the day when they would become naturalized citizens. Most had jobs working for less than nothing, yet they were able to send money home to Italy. I remember the onions, peppers, and sausage sandwiches and the smell of saltwater.

The midthirties were coming to an end. I was seven years old in 1936, and I had a lot of freedom. I was able to roam the streets in the middle of the night. My mom and dad were fast asleep, dreaming that one day I would be a great doctor, but at seven I knew I would be a thrill seeker. I slept in the living room, and my mom and dad had a room in the back of the house. The kitchen was the largest room in the house; it had a great big cast-iron stove. The icebox was kept cold by a block of ice.

My brother was ten years older than me and was living in New Jersey. He had a job working in a grocery store. My brother came home on weekends with a bag of food. I would sit on the stoop and wait for him. Once I got sight of him, I would run as fast as I could to help him carry the food.

My brother had a nice way about him. He and my sister were born in Italy and remained in Italy until my dad became an American citizen. My family spoke Italian. My mom had a tough time speaking English. Mom would speak in Italian, and I would respond in Italian.

My room had a stand-up piano with foot pedals. As I struck the keys, the hammers struck the chords, and the music was loud and clear. Dad nailed a box to the frame of the window, and at night the food would freeze. It made no difference; we ate it anyway. Many nights I would climb out the window when everyone was asleep. The back of the house had a garden. It also had a garage that was a shack with a pigeon coop on top.

All the homes faced the street on Euclid and Hageman Avenue. They were perpendicular, and I was able to look at the backs of the two-story homes of my neighbors. Standing on the coop allowed me to see inside most of the homes. The nights were hot, and the windows were wide open. Some neighbors were asleep, and others were walking to and from the bathroom. In one of the homes, the refrigerator door opened, and the light illuminated the hot, shiny body of a nude woman. That was my first X-rated film.

Some women in the neighborhood were hot enough to start a fire without striking a match. Those I kept an eye on. I became a seven-year-old Peeping Tom. People were more interesting when they felt free to act without the scrutiny of others. I was a shadow that moved from one window to the next. At first the dogs barked. A neighbor used his flashlight to see what was stirring up the dogs. I wanted to get closer and zoom myself in to see the breasts that turned me into an animal.

The deadbeats ran wires to the electric poles. For all I knew, water could have been flowing through those wires. I yanked on the wire to see if it would support me. I wanted to swing to a nearby shed. I swung, and a great ball of fire caused the lights to go out. I had to dodge the rays of light as the neighbors were trying to seek me out. The summer months were great, and we did things a ten-year-old would not be permitted to do today.

I entered kindergarten when I was five. I remember going with my mom to school. I knew I hated school. A child walked over and took my hand to play with him. I pushed him, and he fell and started to cry. The teacher told my mother to take me home and punish me! I went through three grades and knew less than when I had started. I was held back, and that was a mistake. Now I could kick the shit out of all the kids in my classroom.

Each day I had to take my sister and a few neighborhood kids to school. We had to walk through the swamp; it was a narrow path. We came to a car that was parked off the path. A man was seated behind the wheel of his car. I jumped on the running board and blew the horn. He did not wake up. My sister told me to get off the car. The kids were moving on. I saw flies were on an open wound that the man had. I took my pencil, stuck it into the wound, and pulled it out. There was blood and brains on my pencil. I took off running, caught up with the kids, and wiped my pencil on one of the kid's shirt. No one told the teacher there was a dead man sitting in a car.

When we went home for lunch, I told my mom there was a dead man sitting in a car. She told me to leave him alone and that he might be sleeping. I told my mom that I blew the horn. Mom said, "He might be deaf." Could I tell Mom that I stuck a pencil four inches deep into his skull?

If you wanted to get rid of someone, the marsh was the place. It was a hit man's cemetery. Just think. You don't need to buy a tombstone. Some hit men got lazy and let the maggots do the work. The mob in the old days had to call for a sit down to stop the killings long enough to let the stench of death dissipate so people could get a breath of fresh air.

As a kid I was nutty, and when I got older, I cornered the market. I loved who I was, and I had a choice: have fun now or apply myself to the task of mental torture. I realized that with my outlook, I was doomed! I had no one to explain to me how to achieve mental health through an interesting, mind-challenging education. To sit in a chair and be bored to death was not my cup of tea.

To break up the bullshit, I would tease the girls. I found myself under the teacher's desk, and that's where my real education began. I explored my teacher, and each day I managed to earn my place under her desk. I was delighted to play a game with a woman who managed to perform in a way that made me think it was a puppet show.

From the window of the school, I was able to see a vast area of swamp grass. Ditches were dug in the form of a grid. I wanted to run and swim in the waters that flowed in and out. As children from Euclid and Hageman, we crossed Linden Boulevard, which divided the wet lands from the dry lands. When the tide was at its lowest point, we would run as fast as we could, trying to catch eels that were trapped in small pools of water. As the tide rose to our knees, we swam with the current. The marshland stretched for miles.

Before Kennedy Airport, there was an airport called Idlewild. It was small and serviced small planes. People from that area had homes along the canals, and they were able to fish from their balconies. The community was alert to strangers. Most of the people from that area were Irish. The Irish would throw stones as we passed by their balconies. We learned fast that we were persona non grata. There was plenty of land for everyone. You could be as prejudiced as you wanted to be.

The marsh ran along the shoreline to Coney Island; many times we would camp on the shoreline and swim in the waters of Jamaica Bay. The marshes were dumping grounds for weak or sick horses. At that time, horses were used for everything, and many died from being overworked. I watched as someone would cut into the vein of a horse. As the blood ran out of his vein, he weakened and fell to his death. I was surprised that there was no pain. The nuns had me believing that death was painful. I came by each day to see what my destiny would be. Within days the maggots were aided by the sun to devour the horse. I used a stick to stir the maggots around. The smell of decaying flesh did not deter me from seeing it to the end. It was not a pleasant thought picturing maggots eating me, and I wanted to get even with the maggots. It didn't take long to find a dead horse. I waited till the horse was covered with maggots.

Mr. Bordino, who was a neighbor, had a junk box for a car. I always used his car for a gas station. I drained a gallon of gas, went back to the swamp, poured gas over the horse, and set him on fire. The maggots appeared like tiny souls burning in hell. I hoped the nuns were wrong about hell.

The marshes on my side of Linden Boulevard were different. They were dry. There were patches of sand dunes, swamp grass, and fertile soil to grow vegetables. There were acres of land that people took for their own personal use. Most plots were less than a half-acre. Fences were built with the debris that was dumped by trucks. Most families allowed their children to escape the heat of their homes.

As we sat on the stoop, the older fifteen-year-olds told stories that kept us in a state of fear. They talked about war and the need to train so we could defend the country. They talked about equipment and the need to build a fort. When they said fort, I immediately wanted to start building. Everyone had a wheelbarrow in those days, and the broken sidewalks were perfect! Trucks dumped load after load, and we all pitched in. Each and every day the wall was rising. The grayish sidewalk made it look like a real fort, and it stood at least three feet high. Our next move was to erect a cross. The rubble was our lumberyard. As the cross rose, we knew we had to defend it. It was the Depression. I would listen to how bad it was, but a gang of kids ate better than our families. We would raid the farms for peppers, corn, and potatoes. With the chicken coops and the pigeons, it was dinner time. Like the Bible said, we reached out and plucked the fruits of others.

(His reverence Al Capone.)

The big guys were Tony, Andy, Johnny, and Mario. The little guys were Tony, Sunny, Johnny, Joe, and me. Andy was the storyteller. He told stories as we sat around eating roasted potatoes.

There were small farms everywhere. Some had sheds on their plot of land. People came at night from the nearby homes looking to buy hot sausage sandwiches. The old guys made homemade wine. We listened to the sound of Caruso singing as we ate. This confiscated land was magical, and the night skies were brilliant with stars. At night the mosquitoes were upon us, sucking the blood from our veins. We made mosquito repellent using a number-ten can, which enabled us to twirl it above our heads. The wind kept the fire alive, and the reeds produced the smoke. The kids big and small were twirling cans. As we walked along the street, it was quite a sight. On Labor Day we all pitched in gathering lumber. No one was safe. We tore down the wood fences, and the old men tried to stop us. They soon were faced with well-trained rock-throwing eight-year-olds.

We placed cannons in a row and drilled a small hole into a milk can. Then we placed black powder into the cannon. We lit a reed and shoved it into the hole, and then came the blast! The cover went for a ride. At times the cannon would split open. This was caused by too much gunpowder.

The wood pile was lit. A bonfire was raging. The people were having a good time.

My dad worked on Wall Street; one of his coworkers cut his throat. My dad lost nothing. The few dollars he made went to the family. Most Americans had no jobs. Times were hard, and food was scarce. We had many friends from Sicily who lived close by. We grew tomatoes in the open fields, and we had a mountain of tomatoes. The kettles were huge, and the fires burned for days until all the tomatoes were cooked.

We had enough to share because we preserved the tomatoes. My dad would go to Long Island looking for wild mushrooms. On many nights my father and his friends gathered around the kitchen table. There were guitars and mandolins, and the women danced on the table with their dresses blowing in the wind. I would stick my head between their legs, and everyone laughed. I feasted on their legs, and that made me nuts.

At the edge of the swamp was a power plant with a smokestack at least fifty feet high. The plant was abandoned for many years; it was stripped of all its machinery. All the pipes had been cut, and whatever made it run was gone. The smokestack at its base, where you took out the soot, was blocked up. Joe's father had a sledgehammer. The plan was to break open the cement barrier to see what was inside the smokestack. We opened the base and crawled in. It was black as night. All we could see when we looked up was a ring of light. To get to the top, we had to climb using the rungs that were cemented into the smokestack. From the outside you could see a platform that was built around the top of the smokestack. I said we could make a club on top of the world. I started up the steel ladder that was full of soot, and it rained down on my friends. They decided to back down, and I started getting scared! When I looked down, it was black. They were outside calling for me to come down, but I kept climbing.

The ring of light was getting bigger; I made it to the top. I looked out, and I could see Jamaica Bay and Coney Island. I stepped down onto the platform; my friends appeared to be two feet tall. I wasn't afraid and started down. The rungs were secure, and I felt confident! I knew we could go up or down with no problem. I told my friends it was easy and that they should just climb and not look down. With that, one by one, we made it to the top. We spent many hours looking at the magnificence of the swamp grass and Jamaica Bay. It was breathtaking.

On weekends we would invade the swamp, looking to swim. When we arrived at the old hole, where most of the ditches converged, the big guys, upon seeing us, yelled to throw us in. We tried to get away, but they grabbed us and flung us into the water. Each kid had to swim for his life. The big guys kept an eye on us and made sure we were close to drowning before they gave us a hand. Once we made it to shore, we were allowed to rest for a while. Then they took us one by one by the feet and hands and swung us back into the water.

The tide was receding. I was the short one, and once the tide dropped to where I could touch the ground, then the big guys left. I was able to swim, since I spent a lot of time practicing on my own. I would gather hermit crabs and put them in my undershirt. We also caught eels, but I wanted hermit crabs. I had a plan.

There was a man who lived in a two-story house, Mr. Bordino, who was a carpenter. He was a big man and a brilliant speaker who loved to make speeches if you broke his window or threw a stone at his home around the time he was having dinner. He always had a late dinner. Most people had eaten and were sitting on their stoops gossiping when I threw a rock at his house. The noise drove him to the balcony. Every man, woman, and child was out in the middle of the street applauding the sight of Mr. Bordino. He exploded into a tirade and cursed the ancestry of the person who threw the stone at his home. His emotions and gestures were not an act. That was pure hate that came from the soul.

The next day I put the hermit crabs into the backseat of his car. The heat of the day turned the fluids from the crabs into an adhesive. The stink was debilitating. The sad part was that he had only one suit for marriage and for death. I loved Mr. Bordino, but I just had to get him fired up. Without Bordino, things would have been very dull.

Another winner was Mr. Cut Nose, who lived across the street and a few homes away from Mr. Bordino. He found a reason to beat his wife every day. I was friendly with his son. They lived upstairs in a two-story house, which was littered with pots and pans. One day it was raining, and I wanted to spend some time with the boy. Since it was raining, the water was coming through the ceiling, and the pots and pans were overflowing. The boy and I had umbrellas, and we would be running around kicking pots and pans.

His mom was something out of a Dumpster. She was a bad reason to be pro-life. Her legs had veins the size of a garden hose. My friend's mother was a beast, to say the least, and at times I would be behind her when I went up the steps. I had a bird's-eye view of a vein that ran up her leg and into her ass. At that moment I was in a direct path of an onslaught. I had to step down a few steps in case she ran out of blood. I always had a hard on around women. Around her I had a half-inch scar where my prick was. I had a vision of Cut Nose on top of her making shit babies. The only time she showered was when it rained.

Directly across from Mr. Bordino was a World War I soldier. It was the Fourth of July, and I was throwing firecrackers through his window. The soldier in his uniform came out with a rifle, looking to shoot someone. Everyone ducked for cover when he took a couple of shots into the air. As he was standing in the middle of the street, I noticed his knickers had a huge bulge in one of his pants legs. About that time, someone tossed a rock at him. The poor bastard ran into his apartment. Some were talking about burning him out, but what stopped them was a lady with a kid who lived above him.

The next day I looked into his apartment and saw him walking around with his balls hanging down to his knees. I was interested in seeing what he had laying around since I never saw him leave the house. I decided to ask if I could see his uniform. He said no, so I told him I had a barrel of wine. He thought about that and said, "Bring me some." I went home, filled up a milk bottle with wine, and gave it to him. He let me in and showed me his army stuff from World War I. He had German helmets, pistols—all kinds of stuff. I started giving him wine, and after a while he would conk out. I would leave with a few things, and when he saw things disappearing, he told me to stay away. He needed wine, and my dad made the best wine in the neighborhood, so I went home to fill up a bottle of wine and pissed into the bottle to top it off. I was teasing him from the window when he grabbed it and downed it.

He asked me, "Did you do something to the wine?"

I said, "It's getting close to the bottom of the barrel."

I fucked with him so bad that he started getting flashbacks. He would look at me and scream, "You fucking Hun."

On the day he died, I opened the window and hopped into the bedroom, looked him over, and thought the piss must have got him. It was time to leave. The shit was driving me out of the house. I was thinking, *His balls would have made a great sack for hermit crabs.*

Breaking windows was my specialty, and anybody who squealed on me got the rock treatment. A lady not too far from where I lived grabbed me by the hair and was slapping the shit out of me. I broke loose and took off, looking for rocks. I got my hands on a couple. I spun around, and she was taking off. I chased her, but I was losing ground. I stopped, took aim for her head, flung the rock, and watched it in flight as the rock curved down toward her head. She stopped and turned to see where I was and ducked just in time to evade the rock. I kept up the chase, and she managed to outrun me. She ran all the way to my father's barbershop to tell my father that I was trying to kill her. The only thing I learned was to make sure not to miss the next time.

My first job was working in a gas station where the owner taught me how to fix flats. I was fascinated about anything to do with a gas station. The owner had a very beautiful wife who would sit in a chair and look at me struggling to move a truck tire. I could not understand why my heart was beating so fast every time I looked at her. She cracked her legs open just enough for me to see her flaming red hairs. She had the whitest legs I have ever seen. She had one eye on me and one eye on her husband.

She was a master of deceit, and like my teacher, she was able to keep me in a state of lust. I had no way to relieve myself. My prick was always hard. The mechanic took notice and called me "little hard on." Every time he called me little hard on, the woman would laugh out loud. I was sure the mechanic was stabbing the shit out of her. Between the two of them, I had my hands full. One day the mechanic asked me if I jerked off. I said, "Yes but nothing comes out." He told me to do it every day, and I made that a full-time job. Once I started popping, I managed to get control of that little bastard.

I was dying to drive a car. My father knew I was fixing flats at the gas station. One night I climbed out of the window when everyone was asleep. I walked around the house and let out the air from the tire. The next day Dad gave me the keys to fix the flat. My dad had a hand pump, and the car was ready to go! Whenever I took a ride, I would watch how

Dad shifted the gears. I would back the car out of the garage and pull it in and out, over and over. To get out, I had to drive the car through the dry marsh to get to the main road. Once I was on the main road, it was Katie bar the door.

I asked the mechanic how to start a car without the key. He showed me how to use the jumpers and a coil. I jumped the starter, and I was on my way. During the day, six of us would take a spin around the neighborhood. The hood had potholes that were a foot or two deep. One old lady lived on the other side of the street and knew me well. The simple reason—I was the one who was stealing her chickens. She was crossing the street, and as I was rounding the corner, the car dug deep into a pothole. She fell into a pothole, and until this day, seventy-four years later, I don't know if I missed her or jumped over her. She went to the barber shop and told my father the story. When he came home, he asked about what the lady said. I told him that she hated me because she thought I stole her chickens. My father was convinced I was telling the truth because he thought I couldn't reach the pedals. Mr. Bordino, my personal gas station, caught me siphoning his gas. I had no defense. I smelled like low-grade gas.

In the swamp there were lots of dairy farms. Horse stables, riding academies, and shanties were within a mile of my house. I loved being around the dairy farms. I was nine when I started to go there. The smell of horse shit and cow shit made me feel strong. Gill, the owner, gave me a job. He took one look at me and said, "You look like a good shit man." Gill gave me a job shoveling shit into a great big cement barrel. There were kids hanging around throwing shit at each other. After the shit fight was over, I would walk on top of the barrel. It was eight inches wide.

I got so good that I was able to run around the top. I tried to get the kids to see how easy it was. They hopped up and started walking around as they followed me. I picked up the pace and caught the last kid. He was around eight years old, and I pushed him in. I was wondering when he was going to come up. He was moving his arms like he was swimming. He started twitching, so I jumped into the shit. There was at least three feet of shit in there, and I was only four feet tall. I created a wave of shit, and he disappeared. I reached down, grabbed his hair, and pulled him up. He was smart enough to keep his mouth shut and dumb enough to keep his eyes open. He had blue eyes when he went in but shitty eyes when he came out.

Gill barred me from the barn. I told him my brother was going to kick the shit out of him. Glenn was a worker who milked cows and said, "Gill, don't let him get a reach on you. He's an Amboy Duke."

The next day I was shoveling shit in the same spot when Gill spotted me and said, "I told you not to come back." I looked at him and said, "I stopped that kid from burning down the barn." He got the message.

The schools had to release the kids so they could get religious instruction. The church was located in an area that at one time was a cow pasture. The church was below street level. It was a small barn before it was converted to a church. The property was at least ten acres square. In the center of the acreage was a pole. The pole was at least ten feet higher than the average electric pole; the church was close to the perimeter. The front faced the open lawn. The street separated a row of homes from the church properties. The acreage of the church property was surrounded by small-sized homes. The pole was in the center of the church grounds; it could be seen by thousands of people. The slope, which ran from the elevated street to the church grounds, enabled the throngs to sit and view the festivities.

St. Geraldo, the patron saint, was honored by the good people of St. Fortunata, a Catholic church. On the day of the feast, people were erecting stands with food and games. The pole was dressed up with a crown of food, to be plucked by a member of the church. The prize was recognition, food, and a small amount of money. Months before the festivities, as I walked with friends to the church to receive religious instruction, I would climb the pole to get practice. It wasn't long before the pole was cleansed by me going up, and down. The nuns were looking from the rectory window. As I was flying up the pole, I would wave at them, and as I hit the top, they let out a holler.

On the night of the feast, the main event was the climbing of the pole. I was looking up at the crown of food, the night stars, and the lights from the food vendors. Two little girls were hanging between the electric poles; they were harnessed by straps. The ten-year-olds were speaking in Italian and dressed up like little angels. I looked up at their white wings and thought, *Soon I will fly higher than them.* The main event was getting close to the start of the climb; the crowd was moving to the slope, close to the greased pole. I pushed my way into the inner circle, looking for someone who would take me for a partner. There were five couples that had cleaned two-thirds of the pole. I was about to jump on the pole when one of the men shoved me. I went down, jumped up, and grabbed a few sacks as soon as they came down.

I leapt on the pole and up I went, truly a monkey. As I was climbing, there was a great roar. The people were screaming. I stopped, let my feet dangle, and then continued to climb. I hit the spot where the grease was and started to clean. The crowd was screaming for me to come down! I took a handful of grease and flung it out into the crowd. One of the men came up and said that I had won, and I said, "I wanted the salami." Before he went down, he let me rest on his shoulders. Then he put both hands on my ankles and slid down the pole. I was kicking my feet to disengage myself from him, but it was to no avail; his weight forced me down. As I hit the ground, I was picked up and thrown from one person to the next. I was ecstatic and had never felt such pride. I had accomplished something. I felt my life had meaning!

To my delight, I was carried to the stage and stood before the throng. I said that I had to prove to those who tried to stop me that I was just as good as or better than them. The neighbors knew me as a fuck up who needed to be watched. Breaking windows was still fresh in their minds.

My older sister came with me to pick up the groceries and the money. The Sisters said we were only entitled to the money and that they wanted to keep the groceries. My sister insisted that the groceries be included, and she was face to face with the nuns. She did not blink an eye, and the nuns relinquished everything.

A few of my friends were tagging along, taking bites out of the salami. With the money, I bought a new bike. From where I lived to Rockaway Beach was a good ten miles. All the kids in my neighborhood had secondhand bikes, and we took the bikes to undreamed of places. One was the beaches of the Rockaways. One of my favorite pastimes was walking under the boardwalk, looking up the skirts of women. Most women were without panties. The place we liked the best was where the bathrooms were. It seemed that they did a job on themselves. I was all eyes. Some women had bushes that looked like Christmas trees, and others were shaved. I liked those the best. I saw cracks that were zigzagged and others that were open; no matter what, I enjoyed each and every one of them.

I managed to run along the beams jerking off. There were a dozen of us playing with our dicks, and at times we would be calling to each other to look at this one or that one. When someone got a hold of a hot one, we would push each other off the beam. We were able to run on the beam as if we were in the Olympics. At times the women knew we were looking up at them, and they would pour water over us. It was great. The best time was when a hottie was walking by with the biggest balls I had ever seen. It took a while to figure that one out.

I was always on the lookout for a pair of pants that were hanging on the fence, which ran parallel to the boardwalk. We waited for the guy to head for the water. His girlfriend was reading and keeping an eye on his pants. I told Charlie and Joe to start a fight. She stopped reading and was paying attention to see if there was going to be a fight. I sneaked up to the fence, took the wallet, and crawled away. We hit the jackpot with fifteen dollars, a week's pay.

We hit the rides and went to Irish town. The Irish girls were dressed in costume, and the music was delightful. The dancers were slim, self-confident, and hard to rattle. Nevertheless, when one dancer passed by to take a break, I told her that she was great and a wonderful dancer. She took a long look at me and asked what my name was. I told her Mike Cassidy. He was my favorite cowboy. She asked me where I lived; I said I lived in the marshes on the other side of Jamaica Bay. She smiled and said that she also lived in the marshes in Broad Channel, which was just a couple of blocks past the bridge. She told me to wait because she had a few more dances to finish.

I waited and was falling in love with her. It didn't take me long to flip over a good-looking girl. She had finished dancing and came back and asked me to walk her home. I was extremely dark from the sun, and my eyes are somewhat blue. She said she wished she was dark as me. My friends left to hit the rides, and I took my bike and we withdrew. I told her about the greased pole and that I'd won the prize and that I had bought the bike with the money. We crossed the bridge and walked a few small blocks to a catwalk that led to a shanty on stilts. The canal ran beneath her shanty. I left my bike and walked to the porch with her.

Her father and a few others were drinking beer, and they took a look at me and were smiling from ear to ear. He said to his daughter, "What are you doing with a black wop?"

She seemed stunned. She told him that I was Irish and that my name was Mike Cassidy. They all laughed at me. I was too sad to be angry; I knew right then and there that I had lost the prize. She looked at me and asked, "Are you Irish?"

I said, "No, I'm just a black wop."

I turned and walked away, listening to the catcalls. As I walked away, I understood that it's like that old movie, look what the cat brought in. I walked a few miles, got on my bike, and promised myself not to think too much about it anymore.

I started hanging around the beach quite often, and the money was rolling in. The elevated trains took us from the beach to New York City. Most of the time we went to the movies. We visited the Statue of Liberty, and we climbed the steps of the Empire State Building. The first time we were there, we were above the clouds, and it was an awesome sight! It was like I was in heaven, and that was about the closest I'll ever get to heaven.

At that time, there were no barriers, and we would sit on the wall and throw pennies. People would tell us not to do it because a penny could kill someone. I knew for sure they were stupid. There was no way a penny could kill anyone. I would scream, "I'm a dead-end kid," and "I'm on top of the world." I honestly believed that the dead-end kids rewired my brains and I was doomed by a sickness that made the forbidden fruit my favorite fruit.

Cops on the beat were on the lookout for kids who were stealing wallets. There were around six of us. The playground was not too far from the police station. A cop in plain clothes started to talk to us about where the money came from. I told him that I shined shoes.

A year before most of us worked on a fruit truck hustling fruit and vegetables. The Morgan Brothers had a few trucks, and we covered the cabanas. We had to get rid of all the vegetables that were on the truck, no matter how long it took. There were four of us, plus the driver. After two weeks working, we knew the ropes. When the day was over, we had to take off all our clothes, and we were thoroughly searched. I made it my mission to try and beat him for all the money I could get. I managed to get my hands on a couple of dollars a day, which was a huge amount of money. When I caught a live one who had too much to drink, I would overcharge him or her. I took the dollar bill, rolled it into a tiny ball, and shoved it up my ass.

The cop said, "I'm taking you kids in," and then walked us to the police station. I had been in that police station at least a hundred times, and I knew the cops by name.

The sergeant looked at me, and said, "He looks like a thief but is a hard-working kid." The donkey said that if he ever saw us under the boardwalk, he'd run us in. One of us said as we walked out, "Fuck you, donkey," and we ran out the door, over the bridge and walked home.

In school things were the same. I was fucking up bad. The girls liked me, and at times, when I came into the classrooms in the morning and placed our clothes in the closet, they would allow me to feel them up and kiss them on the mouth hard.

I knew a few kids from Canarsie named Charlie, Muzzy, Joey, and Tony. The kids all lived around the Canarsie shit canal. There was an outpost for soldiers who were defending Floyd Bennett Field. It was an airport that had dummy airplanes. The outpost was nearby, and they had antiaircraft guns. The soldiers and their wives lived in Quonset huts. The soldiers were so drunk that their wives were selling pussy on the side while they were sleeping. The defenders of America were rounded up and shipped overseas. One week later the wives were using live ammunition for dildos.

On a breezy day you could smell hot pussy, despite the proximity of the shit canal. We, the dirty dozen, moved in and started knocking on doors, asking where the soldiers were. A woman opened the door, and I knew we'd hit the jackpot. She had three kids hanging on her, one filthier than the other. I watched with fascination as one child was sucking her tit.

I asked her in jest, "May I suck your other tit?"

She answered, "Do any of you have whisky?"

I told her that my dad had a wine barrel. Between the six of us, we managed to pony up two bucks for some Sneaky Pete.

We named her Whiskey Rose. She was a born-again whore. We wanted to throw a party, and we asked her if there were there any hot-to-trot wives hanging around. She sent her snot-nosed kid out to round up some of the ladies while Charlie, Muzzy, and I went to a grocery store that was close by. After we went in, Muzzy kept the store clerk busy while Charlie and I stuffed our shirts with baloney and cheese. Muzzy paid for the Sneaky Pete. When we got back, the party was on, and the girls were all drinking from the gallon. Whiskey Rose was a natural-born drunk, and the girls wanted a live dick! We all stood on top of the table, and the girls stood on the chairs sucking away. Whiskey Rose had three teeth, and when she bit down, it was like three hypodermic needles sending a message to yank my dick out. Like greed, pain is good.

I graduated grade school, went to PS 202, and was put in a class at the highest level. I entered the class and found out that the students and the teacher were Jews. I took my place after the teacher handed out paperwork, and then he asked me to introduce myself to the class. I said my name and then wrote it down but spelled it wrong. The teacher said that I had written my name wrong, and the kids were laughing at me. I rewrote my name as Batman, and the class went wild. The teacher told me to write my name right and I said, "Fuck you." The class went dead quiet. The teacher was taking me to the principal's office but then changed his mind and asked me a few questions about my background. I said that I had a job working on a coal truck in the summer, and after school I made cement blocks. He was in shock. He told me to try my best and that he would get someone to help me.

I sat it out for a year trying but not knowing math, grammar, or spelling. And then there was the call of the wild. I left the class with a different view of Jews, their relentless pursuit of knowledge, and putting up with me. I was placed in a class that was loaded with clowns like me. Now I could function, but that was my last chance. I was ashamed of myself, and I turned to violence. I was strong; I was working with men who were brutal in nature and quick to explode. They gave me an insight about what it took to defend yourself. I was a kid, and so I was lucky that I could shoot off my mouth and get away with it. Some were not so lucky. The liquor, the confrontations, and the knives plunging into men were a sight I will never forget.

The cops would come and look at these men in amusement, not caring who won or lost. It was all the same to them. I'm not saying that all cops are the same. A lot of them kept a step or two away from actual danger. Who would want to step into a fight between two titans who had super strength?

The coal business taught me to strike first in a fight. The only class I liked was shop, and I enjoyed working with tools and wood. I told my dad about the wood shop. It was the first time I had said something positive about school. He told me to fix the pigeon coop because the pigeons were coming and going on their own. I told Charlie to give me a hand, and we busted into a lumberyard in the neighborhood to get some boards. It took us a few days to gather all the wood we needed, but what we needed now were tools.

The teacher, Mr. Ford, told us to put away the tools before we left. I managed to open the window and toss the tools out. The next day while I was walking to my class, the principal yelled, "Castello. You are under arrest."

He marched us to his office and questioned us about the tools. I knew who had told on us; it was a classmate. He was standing in front of the office and shaking badly. No one said a thing. The principal sent for my dad. When my dad arrived, the principal told him what I had done. My dad stepped in front of me and asked me if I had done it. I said nothing, and he slapped my face as hard as he could. I never moved. He repeated it several times, and looked at me and I smiled. I could see that I had beaten him. He told the principal, "I can't hit him anymore. My hand hurts."

Dr. Ike picked up a Bible, placed it against my face, and said, "God wants you to change. Do you believe in God?"

I said yes! I knew that I had shamed my dad. I was crying uncontrollably. I remember the principal saying that the only thing that made him cry was the mention of God. "The only thing that keeps me from changing to a Christian is that I'm a devout Jew."

I was working with the Varia brothers, and they had a coal, and cement block business. One of the brothers had a 1923 Mac Bulldog, chain-driven dump truck. It took thirteen yards of coke ash. The ash was shoveled onto a conveyor belt. The work was hard and back breaking. We took the loaded truck to his home, where we dumped it on his property, which was at the end of the marsh. His father used the ash to make cement blocks. The son also used the truck to collect stones for the cemeteries.

We would go out into the fields to locate big boulders, and using chisels, we would find a vein in the boulder. Then with a sledgehammer, we busted the boulder into smaller pieces. I would carry the smaller pieces to the truck, and Jimmy would load it. Each day was the same process until the truck was loaded. The stones were used for the foundation of the tombstone. The work was hard and not very much fun.

Whitey's brother, Paul, had a Bulldog Mac chain drive, ten-ton coal truck with a crank handle to start the truck. I had to practice standing on top of a milk box to spin the crank and start the engine. The fear was that it was easy to break your arm, and if you were slow to move your hand when the engine started, if you did not engage the crank, it would spin like a propeller on an airplane. You had to release it in a split second. Learning to roll a coal barrel took time. A fully loaded barrel weighed two hundred pounds. After placing the neck of the barrel on the chute and then picking up the barrel, you must use your legs to help you lift it up. That builds muscle in your arms, legs, and back. I enjoyed the race we had from the chute of the truck to the basement window.

The winters were tough. I was rolling coal instead of being in school, but the teachers were relieved when I wasn't around. The New York winters, with the snow and the wind blowing, didn't faze me. I loved when the women came out the door wearing fur coats and then seeing me dressed in a sleeveless undershirt, running up and down the driveway! I wasn't much taller than the barrel. Most had to stop and watch.

I loved to look at the older woman, and they knew it. Something about a small, young boy turned them on. Living with a man that had a great big belly was not too pleasant a thought. But a kid who showed an interest in an older woman—especially when he had a hard on while rolling a coal barrel when it was brutally cold—had to turn them on. I never forgot the black girls who lived in the basement apartments in the high-rise buildings who had to stay indoors so they wouldn't annoy the people. The children would be running around in the coal dust. I would be in a coal bin, shoveling coal as it came down the chute. I was twelve when I started with the Varia Brothers, and at thirteen I was as strong as a man. The only sex I'd had was a blow job or a hand job. I started paying the black girls fifty cents to look at their pussies. It was not too long after that that I started having straight sex with them. Since I had money, the older girls took over. I never knew what a pleasure sex could be. The blacker the girl, the hotter I got.

Paul started taking me to nightclubs. He told my mother we were going to the fights. This was the first time that I got a close look at a woman completely in the nude. She came close to the table, and Paul told her to fuck with me. She sat in my lap and made me feel her tits. An electric shock went through my brain. I was very comfortable in this environment.

Tough guys were walking around; there were all kinds of rooms. The mob had a way of knowing what the general run-of-the-mill guys liked, and they had lines waiting to get in the rooms. Paul wanted to know if I wanted to go in one. For one reason or another, I had bad feelings about what was going on.

Paul knew a lot of the women we delivered coal to. If Paul had to take a piss, he would take his prick out and stick it between the wooden spokes of the truck wheel. Once he started pissing, it was like someone opened a spigot. A golden river was flowing. The first time I saw him do that, I could not believe my eyes. He was so nonchalant, like nobody would notice him. I suppose that was his defense for indecent exposure. "But it worked on the women." When they saw the coal truck pull up, they must have been praying for him to take a piss. If he liked someone, and if he knew he had a chance, he would ask the lady to use the bathroom. I'm sure once she heard that piss that sounded like a cop whistle, she was a goner, and the next time we came to deliver coal, she was ready!

The noise she made when she was getting hit by that monster cock was music to my ears. Each day we headed for the coal yard; World War II had started, and the war was hot. But people were cold because the price of coal had gone up. There were long lines, and we had to lessen the amount of coal to each customer. Paul told me to hang out in the diner across from the yard. I wanted to hear black music, and I loved the words and melodies. The blacks that I knew argued to elicit controversy in a very humorous way. I turned it on, and they laughed. I never saw deliberate meanness. I soon spoke the same language. The lady behind the counter egged me on. The woman said the only reason she let me in was because the coal dust made me look black.

At that time, I believed that Italians should marry our own kind. Some people looked at Italians as stupid, dirty people and thought that no self-respecting person would marry one. The thing was, I knew better. I loved my family and my friends, and our only protection was sticking together. There also was a common bond between us, and the reason was, we were in the same boat. The blacks trusted us because at that time, the newspapers sensationalized any crime that was committed by an Italian. They romanticized the doings of the mobsters because it did not concern them. The average American thought that they only killed themselves. The average person could walk through an Italian neighborhood and feel safe. That attitude stigmatized the Italian people to this day.

Paul came into the restaurant and said to me, "Let's go." All our customers were mixed. The Jews found us work. The Jews were only interested in the money. I guess you can apply that to everyone.

I could say quite a lot about my family. Despite all the crap I put on them, my sisters sacrificed quite a lot, and they succeeded in raising families that are very successful. I was the only one who made a living at the point of a gun. The less I say about my family, the better.

Pauly wanted me to go on a blind date with one of his girlfriends. She was a huge woman and had a sister who was huge. Her huge body covered every hole. I had to poke around trying to find a place to put my prick. The only hole I found was in her ear. I decided the only thing I needed was a hand job. If you ask me about looks, there was none. Every time she moved, the flesh rippled, like when you throw a rock into a pond.

I went from a white school to a school where the students were teachers of crime. The classes were bedlam. A teacher, a white Miss Bentley, stood at the front of the classroom speaking in a Minnie Mouse voice. She would shout, "Please don't throw the ink wells at me."

One hunk of black flesh waved his prick at Miss Bentley. She did not know what it was. She shouted, "Come to the front of the class and put that club on my desk." The behemoth had a hole in his pocket, walked up to Miss Bentley, reached into his pocket, and pulled out his cock. Miss Bentley ran out of the room. The only thing she left behind was her shoes.

I rapped like a black, and I had it made. I was teaching them how to steal a car. If you wanted to survive and you were white, the safest thing for you to do was tell fuck stories. Fuck stories were the only thing the teacher had no power to stop. If the teacher tried to stop the person talking about sex, the kids would jump on their desks and start throwing whatever they had in their hands. Books were flying, ink wells were flying, and kids were throwing chairs at the teacher. The fuckups would be walking around pushing fuckups. There was no possibility that the teacher could get anything done. Going to school was exciting.

The subway train was packed with people going to work. Tony was one of my friends from the neighborhood. He had the looks to stop women in their tracks. Every morning going to school, we would meet a young woman in her twenties who was crazy about Tony. He told me that she was playing with his cock. We would be standing in the middle of the subway car, everyone was crushed together, and she would whisper in his ear to put his hand up her snatch. Each day she would get bolder.

We skipped school, she took us to her job, and we hung around. She gave us money, and we went to the movies. When she got done with work, we would ride the subway home. She allowed Tony to enter her and hang on. Sex was a sickness for her. The Bible says you must seek the heat of the loins to cleanse the sickness of the mind. The best teachers of degeneracy were in abundance, and we were surrounded by them. They aided and abetted us. The lady who was in search of child sex ended up being groped by men and women.

Religion will dissolve in the midst of a turbulence that boggles the mind. Those who went to work to bring bread home wound up riding the express train to the gates of insanity. And for that, they worked themselves into a state of insatiability. The express was a fast-moving train that took you to every nook and cranny. One day Tony, a close friend of my family, and I got off the train to go to City Line in Brooklyn to have some fun. It was always a good place to do shopping. There was a lot of activity. Most places were privately owned. There were no big supermarkets that took over everything. If you wanted to get your shoes done, there was someone to fix it, just the way you liked it, and you could bargain with them.

The train station where we got off was in the heart of the shopping center. One incident that took place has to be recorded. Tony and I were walking along, and we heard a loud noise. We knew that it was a car accident. We took off running, and within five minutes, we were at the place where the accident took place. A truck hit the post that was holding up the train track. We looked to see if the driver was hurt, but there was no sign of him anywhere. Within a minute or two, a train drove over the spot where the post was knocked over. The train took a nose dive, caused by the loss of the post. The train continued moving on.

Tony and I ran to the station. We climbed the stairs. Tony was faster runner than I was, and he jumped down on the tracks as a train was coming into the station. Tony took off his shirt and was waving it. As he was walking, the subway car came to a stop. He was standing twenty feet from the subway car. I told the conductor about what took place a couple of hundred feet from where he stopped. We made sure that the conductor knew the situation. It must have been the rush hour, because the train was only ten minutes or so behind the train that caused the collapse of the train tracks.

After that, it seems I drew a blank. I don't believe it would take much to verify this story. I'm not looking for glory at this stage of the game, but it would be nice to know that I did something that really counted. It can't be a dream!

The subway was a magic carpet. If we decided to have lunch, the bars were the place to hit. We mostly frequented the Irish bars. The food was free. The bars pushed drinks. We had to move fast. I grabbed the meat, and Tony grabbed the bread and pickles. Speed was a must, and we took off. The Irish bastards were half drunk and gave chase. One ran into the street and got hit by a car. We managed to escape and headed for the subway cars. Invariably we lost some of the loot.

We decided to head for Creedmoor. After eating lunch on the house, we went from car to car looking for laughs. I spotted a girl sitting there. She had a smile to go along with the dumbest look on her face that said blow job. We had an act that most girls fell for. We argued about how stupid we were. She started laughing, and then we moved in on her. I told her that Tony liked her and that we were going to the nuthouse to have some fun with the screwballs. We asked her to come along because this was dance day. I told her again that Tony liked her. She let out a cry, "Jeepers!"

Tony was fourteen and looked like he was twelve. He was on his knees begging her to marry him. She was on the chubby side but had the biggest tits. The ride to Creedmoor was about a half hour. We got to Creedmoor.

The place was wide open, and the dangerous patients were locked up. The patients were well-dressed. Some had jobs mopping floors. The fun part was that if you asked one of them a question, the patient was happy to oblige. They would drag you from one hallway to another, in one door and out the other.

Soon more patients were joining in. The patients were very excited. They liked Jeepers and were holding on to her. I told Jeepers that the patients liked her a lot and wanted her to stay with them. Tony and I made a dash for the door. Jeepers was surrounded and was screaming for Tony. We took off.

School was a drag. No one asked anything when I wasn't there. One student less was all the better. When I came in, I sat in the back of the class talking shit.

I stopped being aggressive, and I gave up trying to be a mechanic. I asked around the coal yard if there were any trucks for sale. The word was out that I was looking for a driver. Paul asked if I was looking to be on my own. I told him I had a belly full of coal. I was back on the streets, and started fucking up in school.

While I was in class one day, I was throwing spit balls at the teacher's head and hit him. The teacher was fuming and said that only a coward would do that. I raised my hand, and he asked me to step out into the hallway to talk. He was trying to explain that the classroom was not a playground, that it was a place to educate students. A kid was passing by, and I turned away from the teacher and started rapping with him. The teacher turned me around and slapped me, and I instinctively fired a punch to his stomach.

He was a tall man. He bent over, holding his stomach, and we were head to head. Now he was my size, and I wanted to smash his face in. His eyes were filling with tears. He said, "Leave and never come back."

I said, "I want my working papers."

He said, "Come back tomorrow."

I started hanging out at the Brooklyn Navy Yard. Sand Street ran along the waterfront. The bars also ran along the waterfront. At night the lights cast a dark glow. The alleys were dark and forbidden. Nonmilitary types started showing up looking to mug young soldiers, who were looking for a good time before they were shipped out. They all wanted to blow the last few dollars on some whiskey and women. They didn't count on some young kid calling them fags. The young soldier thought that he could kick the crap out of some young punk, not thinking that he was being set up as he stepped into the alley to kick some ass. A well-placed shot to the back of the head with brass knuckles put his ass in dreamland. Once the soldiers and sailors were in the bar and had spent all their money on blow jobs and whiskey, they stepped out into the air and passed out. Whatever he was wearing was gone.

The MPs were a help, but they were undermanned. The action was fast and furious as you walked past the bars and looked through the windows. Seeing the fights that were going on was fascinating. Tables and chairs were thrown through the windows, and it was like spontaneous combustion. Some were hurt badly. The soldiers and the sailors were at each other's throats. The bars weren't called bloody buckets for nothing. I got to know some of the owners and offered my help to clean up after a fight was over. I became an asset. I would have worked for nothing just to see the action.

The girls were tough as nails. Charlie and I befriended them, and they gave us tips. We helped running soldiers and sailors into the saloons. We had an advantage because nobody wanted to kick the shit out of a young kid. Charlie and I would help the MPs dump the sailors and soldiers into the meat wagon. Once it calmed down, the girls were able to suck some prick.

I got to know most of the girls, and it was the same old story. They lived in shanty towns outside of the bases, and they ran away to get out of the house. While waiting for their boyfriends to get off of duty, they spent hours fucking and sucking. Once the guys were shipped out, the girls were on their own. They took advantage of the opportunity, and now they could make some money and find a career for themselves. With all that action and sex, morality ended up in the spittoon. The whore's life was for her.

I asked one girl what she liked the most. She said, "Sucking cock, sucking pussy, and whatever else there is."

I asked her, "With all the cock you sucked, could it be possible that you sucked your lover's cock when you were under the table and you didn't see him?"

She said, "I could still taste the tobacco juice in his sperm." She had a sexy mouth, and I asked her to blow me. She said no and told me that her boyfriend had spies and killed people for no reason whatsoever.

I decided to get a tattoo, and I picked out a bird—a robin red breast. The fuck who gave me the tattoo was drunk, and he cut into me deep. I took the pain and said nothing. A week later Charlie and I waited for him to pass the alley. I caught him on the knee with a lead pipe, and he collapsed. He thought he tripped. I would pass the tattoo parlor, but the fuck never returned.

During the daytime I would hang around the German and Italian prisoners of war camp. The prisoners stood in a fenced-in area. As Charlie and I approached the camp, they would head to the fence. We got to know each other quite well. Charlie and I would charge the fence yelling, "Hail Hitler."

This one kid—and he was a kid—said in English, "What is your name?"

I yelled, "I am Mussolini," and he would laugh.

I approached the fence to look into his eyes. I asked him if he was Catholic. He said no and I told him that he looked like an angel. He stuck his fingers through the fence and touched my fingers. As much as I wanted to get into a war and was confronted by an angel, in my heart I knew that if I had to look the enemy in the eye and see an angel, I doubt if I could have pulled the trigger.

The Italians were more like me, looking for pussy. I started talking Italian, and one guy from Sicily recognized my dialect. I told him that my family came from Musi Melli. We talked, and the subject of pussy came up. I told him to stick his prick through the fence and that I had a dog that sucked prick. He said to me bring my girlfriend around. I picked up some rocks from the street and started to throw rocks at close range. Some got through and hit him. I'm sure that he didn't want to get into a fight with American citizens. That for sure would have put him in real trouble.

They had it made. They had good food and a cot to sleep on, and there was no need to fly off the handle. The yard next to the prisoners was a depot for German airplanes. The wings of one airplane were cut off, but the fuselage was intact. The swastika was blazing, and it was an amazing sight. I had to climb a fence because I needed to get into that airplane. Charlie and I climbed over a huge pile of fuselages. There was one that was in good shape. I climbed into the seat, and I felt like this was the life for me—to be a warrior. The newsreels portrayed the German soldier as a warrior, and I was very impressed. I was fourteen going on fifteen, and my blood was boiling. I felt invincible. There was nothing nice about me. I saw myself as a work of art, speeding into the gates of hell.

The corner was a hot bed of activities. It was a den of thieves. It was the last stop on the IRT elevated line. That's where we would be hanging out. Across the street was another deli, plus a number of stores. The gamblers, thieves, burglars, and hit men seemed to function without work.

The foundations of most men were their wives. The wives managed to hold onto a few things that their husbands came up with. These women were not young, yet they paid off mortgages and kept their husbands' clothes clean, and the men never wanted for anything. They were always on the take. They made sure that the fridge was full. Most were good card players, and they were always looking for a mark. On the fringe of the circle were the card rooms, the Italian American club, the floating crap games, and the Italian lottery. The sharp ones with the sharp wives survived! Strong family ties held them together. Most of the men were kids, and they loved woman. They gossiped like woman, and they were upbeat.

Then there was the Horn He was tall, good-looking, and blessed with a horn between his legs. Women would come from outside the corner, looking to get fucked. They came by train and bus. I saw them go from being thin to fat slobs, sitting at the counter eating bialys. Bernie the counterman kept the girls eating, and he would shout, "Eat or lose your seat."

The Horn was ready to challenge the guy who had the biggest cock. Mickey Legs, a bookie, was taking bets. The Horn took his cock out and banged it on the table to bring it to life. The girls spun around on their seats to get a closer look at his mammoth cock. In the meantime, Bernie slipped in two eggs over easy while the girls were hypnotized. The challenger, Al was six-foot-six and had a chance. He had a cock with varicose veins that popped. Al banged the head of his cock on the sugar bowl. They were ready to duel, and the rabbi got 10 percent for being the judge. His only demand was that they were circumcised. The Horn banged down hard on the sugar bowl to start the challenge; the two pricks looked at each other eye to eye. Al wanted to be measured from behind his balls. His argument was he stuffed his balls into the broad's snatch! The Horn screamed, "Let him throw his asshole in it if he wants!"

The rabbi's eyeballs were locked on the dueling dicks, as he raised his hand, he grasped a serving spoon and struck the head of Horn's horn. The corner never failed to deliver—blessed be the Jew who delivers justice to the few.

Al was fourteen when I met him on the corner. His claim to fame was a deck of cards. Card tricks were his passion. For sure I thought he was retarded. Everything was funny to him. He had a strong thing for religion, and really believed in God. I got him laid, and that changed his life. From zero to ten, God dropped to one. He told me that when she opened her legs, he noticed his cock was four inches longer. I paid the broad that was hanging around two bucks to get laid. The broads were paying Big Al five bucks to get laid. He had a ball-busting job; I told him to quit the fucking job and start his own business. I told him that he could be the business and his cock the tools.

The corner was like socialism. We ate for free. Ninety percent of the working people in the deli were hard up for a piece of pussy. We walked in with a hot chick, and the menu was on the house. The owner married one of the broads, and three blow jobs later, she walked away with half the joint. Blessed be the lame. Al got "good news"—his dad died of aggravation and left him the Caddie. I told Al that he had a gold mine. For starters, he could shoot dice through the open window of the Caddie, play card games, and had a broad to keep the owners of the deli dishing out the food.

Seventy-two hours later, the godfather heard that there was a crime wave going on and sent two hit men down. They caught a guy sucking pussy in the backseat, plus two guys playing cards in the front seat. The hit man knew my father and remembered me climbing the greased pole. He said, "You little mother fucker, you are defying the family. The only thing that is keeping you alive is that you put on quite a show on that pole. That's something I'll never forget. If I have to come back here, I'll burn you alive in that car. Keep the place clean."

The kid shit came to a screeching halt. The corner was wide open, but the cops had three eyes. The sons of bitches could see out of their assholes what was going on, plus it was hard to make a buck.

I was closing in on sixteen when Tony got me a job working in a factory on Thirty-Fourth Street, in Manhattan, and I went for it. The subway ride each morning made my day. When the doors shut, my hands were everywhere, and I sort of bumped into a wallet. Bang, a new career.

For a fist fuck, you have to have the courage to look a woman in the eyes and give her some tongue. When you catch her the next day, get behind her, slip your hand between her legs, and ride her until she starts grinding on the side or your hand with your thumb up her ass. She will pop before you reach the next stop. God will send you to heaven if you have finger-licking fingers. The angels will be waiting for you, no matter how dirty your fingers are.

The job I had was making yarn, and it was the worst in the world. Ninety percent of the workers were Irish. One woman asked me politely if I was a wop.

I told her, "I am an Irish Gypsy, and my name is Mike Castello."

The fish-faced lady screamed, "He's a wop-looking Irish Gypsy."

I got the job going for coffee, lunch, and fucking off. I got fired when I got caught taking a piss in the coffee pot. I never forgot the Cassidy incident.

I needed a license to drive a car; you had to be seventeen to drive a car. I said to Charlie, "Let's go to the church and get a baptismal paper." The priest knew me from the greased pole days, and I told him I needed one to get a job. He obliged, and on the way out, I pressed the button to keep the door open. As he left, I went back in and took a few baptismal papers. A couple of weeks later, I had my license.

I changed my name from Castello to killer on the road. I never loved anything more than a car. I had the power to run over dogs, cats, and people. I spent most of my time hanging around the corner; I had no money. I spotted a guy with a truckload of junk and asked the driver what he got for a load of junk. He ran the numbers down instantaneously. I recollected hot water tanks that were used to fence in the hobo jungles in the neighborhood. Priority number one was to get a car and then a truck.

I knew a crazy fuck named Filthy MacDougal. I used to shoot dice with that guy. He never washed his face. He had a dog whose tongue was pure black from licking his balls and his dog asshole. I asked him about everything, and he was happy to tell me where to sell the junk, who gave the best prices, and which junkyard was easy to bust into. I asked him if he wanted to buy. He said he had no cash, and then I thought maybe he could sell the stuff a little bit at a time. I thought about that. Knowing Filthy, there would be a shootout just to get my end. I conned my dad to lay out the cash. I had a 1932 Chevy in mind, and all I needed was $100. The Chevy had no brakes but had a good motor, and a car with no brakes was a lot of fun. Gearing down kept you on your toes. I was an expert sucking gas out of a tank. Things were looking up. I had the world by the balls.

I got a kid named Sonny to come with me. We hopped over the fence and loaded the car with radiators. I went to a place that took hot stuff. He put it in the press. The price was less, but we came out pretty good. I had to pay my dad off. Sonny and I spotted a fenced-in a yard that had copper rolled up in wooden wheels. Sitting on a platform, all we had to do was back up the truck and load it up. I rented a truck from a friend of mine for a couple of days. The fence gate was open, and we backed the truck up to the platform rolled six wheels of copper on to the bed. Each wheel was very heavy.

I jumped off the truck to check the tires and spotted a cop car coming down toward us. I told Sonny to act like he was rolling the copper onto the platform, and the cop car passed by without a glance. I thought, *One more wheel and the tire will blow.* We took the truck down to the swamp and unloaded it. I poured gasoline over the wheels, set them on fire, and then we sat on the roof of my house and watched the fire burn. The smoke, black as coal, was spreading.

Sonny and I walked over to the site where a cop car was sitting close by. I knocked on his window, and he told me and Sonny to hop in the backseat. The first words out of his mouth were that we smelled like fire. He said, "Give me a c-note; I want to smell like a cop again." This fire was different. The soot was raining down on the clotheslines, and it turned day into night. I tossed him a hundred and asked if he had called the fire department. He said no. A few hours later, the smoke turned white.

All in all we made money. Sonny and I decided to open up a junkyard next to the shit canal, which was in East New York, Brooklyn. We fenced in a few acres of land, the fence being a clothesline. The area was swamp land, and we set the swamp on fire. The fire swept the area, and the next day we roped off the junkyard. The entrance was off a four-lane highway, which was ten feet above the swamp. The road down was good enough, and we were in business.

The best we could do was to steal the cars. Then we had to dig a pit so the bed was even with the road. We took off the tires and battery, drained the gas, and then set the car on fire. The work was hard. Once we loaded a truck, and then as we were taking it to the crusher, a trooper who was giving a ticket to someone saw us drive by. Sonny was driving. I looked at the trooper, and he took a good look at me. I told Sonny to take a right through the neighborhood, the same hood where I almost ran that old lady over when I was a kid.

We entered the neighborhood, and the trooper was blowing his horn. I told Sonny to give it the gas, and the truck started jumping. The trooper got stuck in the middle of a pothole. He was on foot, and he was holding his revolver, a forty-five-caliber, huge handgun, and he fired a shot in the air. We kept on going. The trooper was running and was gaining on us. When we reached level ground, we left him standing in the street. We were on Hageman, heading toward Euclid Avenue, where we turned left. Within a few blocks, we dumped the truck in an alley. We took off on foot and then zigzagged. I was back on Hageman, crossed the street and made it to the front door of my house. I turned the knob to the door, and the trooper grabbed my sweater.

The police officer was as tall as the Statue of Liberty with his arm straight up. My sweater stretched four feet before I left the ground, and I was swinging like a pendulum. Sonny was laughing until the trooper picked him up by the hair. That's one thing Sonny had—hair like iron. Once the trooper calmed down, I asked him if he knew me. He said, "I'll know you when I fingerprint you."

After he let me down, my sweater was still way over my head. He said, "Head for the bike."

A couple of blocks away the bike was sitting in a pothole, and Sonny and I pushed it out. At first I told him my cousin was a detective who owned a bar at the edge of the swamp. He got the bike started, and we walked with the trooper to the bar. The owner said I was the little fuck who used to steal his mother's chickens.

I said, "I told the trooper that you were going to say nice things about me." Sonny was holding his belly and laughing. I said to the trooper, "I'm sorry I fucked up your bike. Let me pay for the damage." I gave him twenty dollars and asked Melo to give him a drink.

The trooper wanted to know where we placed the truck. I told him on Pine Street, and I told him how hard we had worked. The trooper said he was going to pass by to see if we were telling him the truth. We walked back to the truck. The cars were stolen, but he never checked anything. The next day we were back wrecking cars. The policeman would pass each day, and I would put on a show for him, rounding up the burned-up cars. I would smash the, at a high rate of speed, flipping them over and jamming them into the area near the pit. At times someone would be looking into the car that was being readied for burning, and I would be talking shit with him, trying to get him close to the car as I was pouring the gas. At that point, I tossed a match into the car, and the fumes blew his hat off. He ran away with his hair smoking.

Things were not doing too good. There was lots of work but no money. Sonny decided to buy some land in the swamp in the flatlands. I wanted to buy a junkyard in Brownsville in the heart of a black and Puerto Rican neighborhood, and I knew someone who wanted to sell. I took over the junkyard. The junkyard came with seven dogs, and the property had two houses and one garage. A fire burned the two houses down; only the garage, and one room were left. I paid $250 for the yard and $150 for rent. The front and the back were fenced in.

The dogs walked over and introduced themselves to me. Lady, the female, stood in front of me, looked me in the eyes, and started barking like she was talking to me. Lady was the only female. The males were jumping on me. Peoples, the watchman who lived in the office, introduced himself. He was a nice man. He was very quiet, and did things his way. He seemed to have a lot of friends, and they came around when the yard was closed. Peoples had a stove and cooked his own meals. He was used mainly to keep an eye on things. He had a white girlfriend who had one tooth. The office was in good shape. The place had a bathroom and a desk. I sat down and had a good feeling about things. If only I could make enough money to keep me going, it might just keep me out of jail.

I liked to work; I wasn't lazy. In fact, I worked so hard that nobody wanted to work for me. To tell you the truth, I was just an animal. When I had things rolling, I would tell them what to do. They did exactly what I wanted and then waited for the next orders. It seemed like they were afraid to make a mistake. That made more work for me. Each time I had to say the same thing over and over, but as soon as I stopped talking, they stopped working. I found myself doing all the work. All they did was sit around doing nothing. It wasn't that they didn't want to work; it was that they were afraid to work. I've been that way all my life. When I saw somebody sitting around, it bothered me. I didn't have the presence of mind to break them in slowly. I had no patience for that, and it didn't help when Peoples and his friends spent the night drinking.

When I walked in every morning, he was delirious. If I know anything, it's that there's no hope for a drunk. But I did need him at night. I used three of his friends, and I paid them three dollars a day each. I even used Peoples's girlfriend. Sonny was doing well buying old city trucks the city was getting rid of. He would dump and cut up the truck bodies. There were truck bodies all over the swamp. The bums started moving in; they at least had a roof over their heads. I went to Sonny and told him what I needed, and he gave me whatever I wanted. If I had a flat, he told me not to fix it, and he'd give me a good tire. I had at least ten spare truck tires in the yard. He gave me a tow truck and an A frame. With the A frame I was able to pick up cars. Sonny modernized his office and was making good money. I was happy for him and not jealous in the least. I was more interested in getting laid and making a few bucks. Most of the time, I was riding around in my tow truck looking for Puerto Rican women. I did not want to be encumbered with a lot of things that I had no experience in. I was ready for action.

I still had the truck to take scrap to the scrap yard. Everything was set, and I jumped into the tow truck. I cruised the immediate area looking for abandoned cars. Thievery was everywhere. The blacks were on a rampage, and fire trucks were running from one fire to the next. I spotted a cop car on the street, jumped out, and grabbed the cop. I told him I had a junkyard couple of blocks from where we were and that I could clean up the mess. Most of the cars were turned over, and some were burning. The cop told me that I had to get rid of them quick. I told him that I'd give him a fin for each car. He said okay and that he would hang around until I got the job done.

I hooked up a car with one back wheel missing. I told the cop to follow me or follow the grooves in the street. I took off, and the sparks were flying. I pulled into the yard, picked up the torch, and did some chopping and then went back. In the course of the day, I ran five cars through the scrap yard, plus I had a lot of parts to sell. The cops would give me a police escort to the junkers. Most of them were late-model cars and had to be chopped quickly. I put everyone to work. I had one tooth, Peoples's girlfriend, pulling parts off the cars. By the end of the day, Peoples's girlfriend was looking a lot like Sammy Davis Jr. I spread the word to the mob that if they needed an insurance job, to come on down. I did not want a chop shop. My place was wide open. With insurance jobs, I was able to get the title and cannibalize the car. If the auto squad came around, I had the title.

One day Peoples was cooking snouts and ears when the auto squad rolled into the yard wanting a title from one of the junkers. I kept a lot of junkers lying around the yard, and I had titles to all of them. I ran the late models in one at a time with a police escort. I would take the car apart immediately and run it to the scrap yard. I only saved starters and generators. They would take a look at all the junkers and must have thought I was truly nuts. I was saving the VIN numbers on all the late models, which I sold very quickly. I didn't want any hanging around on my desk.

One time I had a VIN number on my desk. While I was looking around for the title of a junker, I spotted the cut-out VIN number. I palmed it and slipped it under a pig's ear. The cop said, "Do you really eat that shit?" I said that that's the only way I get a hard on. I walked out with the detective, and he asked me how I made a living with all that crap I had laying around. He made my day.

I loved to visit the chop shops in the Puerto Rican areas. The girls were hot. By then I was looking like a gypsy. I had a hat with a big tassel on top, sunglasses, and an iron pipe in a scabbard, and I would act crazy.

The Puerto Rican girls were hot. They wanted to get fucked, but they needed money to survive. I generally dropped a five spot to empty my balls. At times they didn't want any money. That was a bad sign because that meant they might be falling in love with you. I didn't want to be caught fucking that girl's sister, especially with my balls hanging low. One time a girl grabbed my balls and yanked my prick out of her sister's snatch, screaming she was going to cut them off and swallow them. I made sure that she took the money.

I must have had at least twenty or so suspects running around, and I was sure half of them must be in jail. Their homes were clean, and they kept themselves clean. They drove their husbands crazy. They were only too happy to get out of the house and go to work just to get away from their wives. In some neighborhoods, every other house was burned out. I noticed children that were jumping out of a window. I was in shock. I got out of the truck and walked up to where they were jumping. As they jumped, they hit a mattress, laughing. I had to go up the stairs to see them actually jump out of the window. All the wood from the steps was missing. The only thing left was a long beam. As I was climbing the beam, a kid was pushing me to go faster. When I got to the top and looked at the kids jumping from the window, I was amazed.

I decided to go into a next room so I could get a better view of the child actually leaving the window and plunging downward, hitting the mattress and bouncing up and onto the concrete. If she had missed, I am sure she would have been critically hurt. I don't believe they thought of the danger; in their minds there was absolutely no danger. If you are fearful by nature, you will see danger in everything. These children were bred in an environment that fortified you against fear. The jump was awesome, and the mattress looked like a bar of soap. There was a five-by-five diamond plate where they burned wood to keep them warm. These kids were not all boys. Some were girls, and they fought each other to get in front of the line. A chill ran through my spine. This was the first time I felt fear for someone else. When it eased up a little, one of the girls who was no more than ten said to me, "You jump." Another first—I felt shit loosen in my ass. I told myself it was time to leave because a few of these kids might be thinking about throwing me out the window.

Don't let me mislead you. It was not easy to roam the streets. This section of East New York was dangerous. You had to fit in. One look at me and they were sure I was Puerto Rican. No one in his right mind would steal from a Puerto Rican unless he was a Puerto Rican. These people demanded respect. I saw a four-foot-tall old lady take a swing at someone who was in her way.

The weather was getting cold. I put Christmas lights on the truck and installed horns that sounded like the cha-cha. I could not pick up any white girls while I was working. The only hope I had to pick up a white woman was at a point of a gun. When I got home, it took me an hour to clean up, and by then I was too tired to go out. I called the yard, and Peoples told me that Buster, our dog, got busted by the dog catcher. We went to the dog pound, and the guy running the show gave me a hard time about how dirty Buster was and said he needed a clean place to live. He was looking at me dressed in rags and carrying a steel pipe. My clothes looked like they had been burned many times because when I used the torch, they would catch fire. I told him I lived in a car and that was my son he was holding. I told him I wanted him now, and if he didn't release him, I would follow him. He handed Buster to me, and I took him home. Lady was very happy to see Buster.

The traffic in front of the junkyard was very heavy, but I never feared for the dogs. Lady would cross back and forth all day long, and the mutts followed her. When I took a break, Lady stood in front of me and barked in different tones. I would question her, and she responded. To this day, I believe that the death penalty should be given for anyone who kills a dog. Lady was free to do whatever she wanted. She had all those dogs sniffing every fart she laid.

It was time for me to move on. The grease was turning me into a caveman. The hood had no McDonalds where you could get a bite to eat or take a piss and wash your hands. I was thinking it might be nice to be a white man again. My net worth was zero. Everything I had was stolen. I passed the word around that the yard was up for sale. The guy who sold me the yard wanted it back. Lady went nuts when she saw him. I told the buyer that I wanted nothing. All I wanted was for him to continue taking care of the dogs and Peoples. I knew the dogs were happy. I gave the truck back to Sonny and left the rest. I then took some time off. I cleaned myself up and went to the Marine recruiting. Then I was on my way to Paris Island, South Carolina.

The trip was by train, which was burning coal. The smoke was black and dirty, and as we went through a tunnel, the black soot would flood the train compartments. We entered the Deep South, going through small towns and open fields. I had a feeling of excitement with this new lease on life. This was my chance to make a career out of the military and maybe, just maybe, I might be in a war. We stopped to let people on the train, and young black boys and girls were selling fruit. Their homes were thirty feet from the tracks. They lived in shacks with Dutch doors. The boards on the homes were spaced two inches apart, and you could see inside. The women were topless, and their breasts would hang way down. It was an awesome sight. The women were walking around dressed in costume like in *Gone with the Wind*. We pulled into Beaufort, South Carolina. We were led off the train and then marched to a convenience store. A marine was talking to several people who were black. They were laughing and carrying on.

Once we were at attention, the marine told us what he expected from us, and then he pointed to the very people who he was laughing with and said, "Do you see those blacks? They are segregated from you, and you are segregated from them."

All the time I watched to see the reaction from the blacks. There was none! They carried on like nothing was said. The marine told us to go into the convenience store and get what we needed.

The training was hard. The marine DIs had come from the Pacific and were battle hardened from the war. I was convinced they saw us as Japanese prisoners of war. The fun began when we started our training. We were taught to march and handle a rifle. One particular DI carried a stick with a lug nut screwed onto it. He would reach into the ranks with it and clip someone on the head. We wore straw hats, and when the lug nut hit your head, the stars came out at daylight. At first the lug nut made a dent and the dent got closer to your skull.

I started to use shit paper by the roll. The DI said to me, "You look like a Jap. You're not as tall as a Jap, but you smell like a Jap, and I'm going to run you out of the corps."

We were at parade rest, waiting to go into the mess hall. Just then, a platoon marched close by, and the DI from the platoon challenged anyone in my platoon to fight with one of his troops. I waited to see if anyone was going to challenge him. I raised my hand and said out loud that I would fight that jug head. I was the smallest marine, and I was in the back. I could have kept my mouth shut, but a challenge is a challenge. I said, "I'll fight the fuck and knock the fuck out. I'm from Brooklyn."

The kid was uptight, and I wanted to knock him out with one punch. The DI from the challenging platoon walked up to me before the fight, and said, "This jug head thinks he can beat my jug head." Then turned to me and said, "I have five Chinese dollars to your five dollars that my boy kicks your ass."

The fight was set for after chow, behind the barracks. They came out with boxing gloves. I said, "No way, we fight bare handed. I don't want to put him to sleep; I want to knock him out fast."

He kept saying that he was the state champ. He was tall and thin, and he was jabbing away at the wind. I was at one end of the circle, and he was on the other. When the platoon leader said go, I ran to him, and he caught me coming in. I felt nothing. I immediately punched him in the face. He backed up and was trapped between the troops and me. I was able to swing freely and was able to connect. He went limp, and he had enough. The DI who was torturing me held my hand up. The way I looked at it, I had beaten two mother fuckers.

I have to say one thing about the DIs, in general. They were funny. The names they called us, the vocabulary they used to curse us out—I looked at that abuse as fun. The training I had from rolling coal gave me the strength of a man. When we finished boot camp, we were given uniforms with the marine emblem. That made me proud to be a marine. We marched alongside Confederate soldiers. I may be wrong on this one, but I was told that they were truly Confederate soldiers. As they marched slowly but proudly, it was an awesome sight as they passed the reviewing stand. Everyone saluted them. You've got to remember, we were in the land of Dixie. The few soldiers who were left did what they thought was right. They did their duty.

Heading home with a two-week furlough was a great honor. Even though the World War II veterans made fun of me, I had the last laugh on them. When the war ended, I was in New York City dressed up in a navy uniform that my friend John, whose brother was in the navy, let me use. The women were going nuts. On Broadway I grabbed one woman who pushed me and said that I was nothing but a fucking kid. Others kissed the shit out of me. I was reassigned to Camp Jejune, North Carolina. I got back to camp, and the next day we had an inspection. Somehow I had lost my duffel bag.

That put me in bad with the sergeant, who was a mean fighting machine. He was built like a monkey. He picked me up with one hand around my neck and said, "Are you one of those black Guineas?"

I said, "No one calls me a black Guinea."

He spun me around, placed me on his knee, and slapped my ass until I felt like he was using a red-hot paddle. He asked me again, "Are you a black Guinea"?

I said, "No, I'm a shit-head Marine."

The jug heads were laughing, and the sergeant called them to attention and said, "If I hear one more giggle, I'll take your pants off and smoke your white asses, and they will look like a red man's ass."

At that I had the last laugh and made a vow that I would make a fool of myself no matter what. I took the most insane chances. Excitement was what I needed to keep me on the edge. I would make a bet that I could raise a hard on in front of twenty guys. I still can visualize them standing there, in my mind conjuring up the sight of pussy. That put me into a trance. My prick would start growing and unraveling, and the guys standing around were transfixed, with their eyeballs sticking out of their sockets.

The best time for me was when we went to the canteen for beer. I had a stack of hillbilly songs. The song sheet had the words in big, bold letters. I started to recite the words, using the mind of a fucked-up head, to put the proper word in the song. I would pour bottle after bottle of beer over my head as I recited the words on the song sheet to express myself openly with no regard for myself. That's what drove me on. It was a catharsis to cleanse my soul of any good thoughts. Those were the days.

There was a guy in my platoon whose name was Birdsong. He was tall, good-looking, and in good shape but a braggart. He always had something to say that pissed me off. I was thinking about washing my web gear when he walked over and asked me, in a nice way, if I would wash some of his gear. I said sure, and he went out. I never washed his or my gear.

The next day he asked me if I washed his gear, and I said that I had forgotten. He had a way of talking like James Cagney, and he called me a shit head. He said if I was a little taller, he would kick the shit out of me. I stood up, picked up my cartridge belt, hit him on the head, and told him to kick my ass. He backed off and said I was too small. I hit him again. He was in shock. The cartridge belt has a brass buckle, and it was heavy.

After that we became friends, but he had to wash my gear and do whatever I wanted him to do. I asked Birdsong if he wanted to go partners on a car. I told him we could score on Carolina beach, and there were no, ugly girls in North Carolina. He thought about it, and then we chipped in twenty bucks each.

We headed for the beach. The weather turned bad, so we stopped at a place called Mom Tiny. The place was jumping. Mom Tiny was a big woman who carried a baseball bat. I asked a redhead for a dance. She said she didn't dance; she just fucked. I liked her looks, and I liked her body. I was dying to see that red pussy.

We went to a back room, and there were twenty guys fucking. The place was rigged with five spigots, each with a six-foot hose. The floorboard had been cut out. The whore straddled the cut out, put the hose in her pussy, and turned the valve on. The blowback caught me in the face. She had a towel and wiped the towel across her pussy. She asked me what I wanted, and I said, "Is there a discount on thirds?"

She had a flaming red pussy, and as soon as my cock got by the double doors, I popped. She rammed the hose into her snatch and blasted the kid out. I took three shots before I could hold back. I was thinking that if any lead got through, I could end up with third-base for a kid. The water pressure ruled out any one-legged Castello running around.

I said to her, "What about some asshole?" She said, "Sure," and rammed the hose in her asshole. A shit storm ensued. "That will be double," she said.

Mom Tiny was like a mom to me. Every time I came in, she would scream and say, "Come over and suck Mommy's tit." She would pick me up and hold me like a trophy. After a year of coming and going to Mom's place, I became a polished degenerate. I even used Mom's asshole for a safety deposit box.

Not too far from Mom's place was a honky-tonk in the woods. Mom said, "Don't go and get yourself killed over there. Stay near the door." As soon as I got through the door, things were hopping. The jukebox was blasting. I asked a girl to dance with me Yankee style. The shed was ten by ten and had a bar. I had some white lightning and gave her a slug. She told me that her husband, who was named Clyde, was carrying a gun and was drunk. I told her again that I wanted to dance Yankee style. Yankee style was when you put your prick between her legs. Somebody told Clyde that a New York midget was dancing Yankee style with his wife. A shot was fired through the ceiling, and Ginger said, "Run! Clyde is shooting the roof off the honky tonk."

Someone screamed, "The midget got a gun," and that gave me time to get out the door. I ran into the night and turned to look. The light on the porch, which was painted black, saved my life. Clyde was sniffing the air to smell which direction the Yankee ran.

I moved on. Mom Tiny, God bless her soul—even though she used me for a dildo, the sweet smell of her pussy will always smell like perfume to me.

We started training for an invasion, and my job was to carry a flamethrower. I was taught to mix napalm with gasoline and practice the art of using wind to enhance the ratio of the kill. I was finally getting an education, something I could put on my resume. The instructor let me direct the stream of death into the wind to let me understand the nature of our job. I almost killed fifteen marines when I used Kentucky wind age and almost turned fifteen marines into Kentucky fried chicken. I was also taught how to use TNT. One day as we sat on a hill, the instructor went through the demonstration on the wiring and the use of prima cord to set off the explosive; we went through the drill over and over.

I got to the point where the only thing I could think about was what would happen if I put TNT into someone's asshole. The place was covered with wires sticking out of the ground. For laughs, I took a wire and tied it to the cartridge belt of the jug head in front of me. I was laughing to myself so hard that I never realized the ramifications of my act. As the instructor said fire in the hole, everyone stampeded. I got up, and the jug head who was trying to get up looked like he was doing a humping movement. He was speechless and tried to get up but was frozen. All he did was stare at the TNT.

The wheels in my demented head were turning. I knew that I would be the number one suspect if he was blown to pieces. I reached down and undid the wire, grabbed him by the collar, and dragged him a few feet. He snapped out of his trance, and we both jumped into the hole. The explosion changed my thinking. I could be a hero. The jug head asked me what had happened. I said, "Don't ask questions. The wire could have been wrapped around your balls."

The fun never stopped. Guard duty was the worst. I knew that Gangbusters was coming on the radio. I loved that program it always came on with a bang. The machine guns, stomping feet, and sirens on the show were to die for. I got a buddy of mine to walk my post. He was a fucked-up Native American who had a drink quite often. I told him that when he got done with the guard duty, we would get together and polish off a pint of white lightning, and he was down for that. An hour went by. Gangbusters come on in the midst of those sirens and stomping feet. As I was lying on my bed, the door swung open. The officer on duty screamed, "Castello, you are under arrest for leaving your post." I was taken to the brig. The case was open and shut. Red Cloud did not have the presence of mind to know that he was in violation of article 1! He decided to discharge a firearm over the heads of two marines and illegally placed the two marines in custody. I was charged with illegally replacing myself with someone dumber than I was and received ten days of bread and water.

The brig was notorious for the brutality they inflicted on the inmates. It was well fortified, and the fence had tower lights. Thank God for Gangbusters. The sight of the brig gave me a warm feeling throughout my body. I was ready for a little pain. Instinctively, I knew that I needed to be tested to become a better man, and I was up to the challenge.

We were placed into cells that had a cot that was on hinges. There was no place to sit. Our punishment was to stand at parade rest all day long in the cell. The MP on duty made rounds, trying to catch someone sitting down on the floor. Each time you were caught laying down, you got a demerit. Five demerits and you got an extra day of jail time. You had a bucket to shit or piss in. Outside the cell was a locker box with a change of clothes and toothpaste. We were fed three times daily, but the bread was moldy. We were given a pitcher to drink from. The first thing on day one was to take the shit bucket, dump the shit down the crapper, and then clean it to the specifications of the MP on duty. If you failed the inspection, you took the pail and had to wear it over your head till lunch time. Everyone in lockup had to take his pitcher to the washroom.

The washroom had over thirty sinks. We had to place the pitcher under the tap and then open the spigot at the same time. The water was pure rust and looked like orange juice. When the water cleared up somewhat, then we shut off the spigot. The reason for this was the rustier was, the better it tasted. After our breakfast of rusty water and moldy bread, we had to put the lock back on the bed. The rules said that every three days you had to get a hot meal at noon.

There was a blackboard with your name on it, plus a star. The days were full of chatter as the MP walked around to see if you were standing. Someone would yell the name of the MP and said that he sucked a black prick. The MP would then open the cells one at a time and have each marine say the exact words. He would go from one cell to another, and when he thought he had the right Marine, he dragged him out to kick his ass and work him over.

We found a way to open the doors at night. When all was done, the sergeant made the final inspection and started to lock the doors with a sliding bolt. He would then go to cell two and work his way down. As he worked his way down, he called out the cell number. The inmate on the back side of the cell block heard the cell number and walked around and opened cell number one and doubled back to his spot. I went to the blackboard and made a star next to my name. I got away with it a couple of times.

To fuck with us, the MP had us use our locker box for drill. He yelled out the cadence, "Left shoulder, right shoulder." I smashed my box into the locker box in front of me, and all hell broke loose.

The ten days went fast, and I got back just in time. I found out that the Eighth Marines, Second Division, were going to Puerto Rico. I was dying to go. The gunny walked into the barracks and said, "Does anyone want to be a barber?" I raised my hand and got the job. I went to his office, and he gave me a box of tools. I asked, "Does anyone want a haircut?" I got a few volunteers. The first sat down, and I took out the hand clipper. When I started to cut, the first squeeze of the clipper got stuck in his hair, and he screamed when I pulled it out. A patch of hair came out of his head. I kept trying, and someone told me I needed oil. I looked into the box, and sure enough, there was oil in there plus a box of white powder. The white powder mixed with oil and blood made his head look like a battle scene.

We went to Morehead City to board a troop ship to Puerto Rico. I had a small barbershop on board. I was opened for business, and my first customer was a captain. He was six foot six, and he said, "Don't fuck up my flat top." At that moment, I felt like Jesus Christ was getting even with me for laughing at the nun when she fell in church. I said, "No problem." He sat down, and I opened the box. I had my forty-five automatic and two hundred scumbags, government issue. In other words, they were stolen scum bags.

I gave him the average haircut—fucked up. What made it worse was that he ended up with a hole on top of his head. He was watching with a hand-held mirror and asked me how long I had been cutting hair. I said, "You are my second customer," and he said, "If this bald spot does not disappear before we get back, I'm going to declare war on you."

We were at sea a few days later. The weather was warming up. A preacher stepped into my shop. Since I always was in a fight, I signed up for the boxing team. I went to the gym and met a couple of Jews from Brooklyn who were a couple of inches taller than I was. There was no one to teach me the ropes. As I was hitting the bag and doing dumb shit, I watched them. They looked good as they moved and jabbed. They would fight each other every day. I asked for some advice, and one said, "Put the gloves on and try to knock me out." He had moves, and as I unloaded on him, he was able to slip each and every punch. I could not put a glove on him. He said, "You are good enough to take on what's around here. Go for the belly."

I was fighting guys who looked like Jack Dempsey. The preacher asked if I would fight after chow on the main deck. The fight was on the cargo hatch, and the ship was jumping as marines and sailors packed the area. I sat in the front. The captain made a speech about a few things, and then he looked at me and said, "This marine fucked up my hair." I wished I was in the ring with him. After two bullshit fights, it was my turn. A six-foot-six black man stepped into the ring looked at me as if I were a child. I was thinking, *Fuck this shit.* He was tall, the ship was rolling, and the captain was introducing us. I was starting to time the roll of the ship.

The sailors and marines were screaming, and we touched gloves. I moved out of range, and he was shadow boxing. He had no idea that it was a real fight, but I was sure this was the real thing. I'm sure he was under orders not to hurt me; he was throwing short punches when I stepped in and hit him in the stomach. He was off balance, and as he went down, his head hit the deck. He was out. The sailors and marines went wild, and I'll never forget that explosion. That moment matched the time; I had climbed the greased pole. The guys hugged me, and every man, woman, and child knew me by name.

Puerto Rico was a God-given place for me. The women were hot and followed us as we walked the streets. Little boys pimped women in their twenties, and the cops could not arrest the children. The girls would pull us into the fields. I was happy. I picked one girl like she was a tomato, and she put rum in her pussy. When I was done, I had six or seven whores. By then, I was drunk and life was good. The harvest was plentiful. Luke 1:7 says, "Blessed is the rum-soaked fruit."

The invasion was on the island of Vegas that was connected to the Virgin Islands and Puerto Rico. We had trained by climbing the net on dry land. I practiced placing shape charges on pill boxes, machine guns, and my trusty flamethrower. What we needed was a war. I wanted to be a hero. I imagined a bronze statue of me, being five foot four, in the nude with a hard on—the kind of hard on that had an everlasting shine.

Gunny was the embodiment of a punch-drunk fighter. He said to me, "If you fuck around on the net, I'll drop a shape charge on your head that will cut off your pistol-grip ears."

I said, "Gunny, at least I won't have to listen to you all day."

On the day of the invasion, we had steak and eggs. I watched as they shelled the island. The planes dropped dummy bombs. It was time to go over the side. The flamethrower had no fuel, and thank God for that, because on the way down, I tried to break the speed record. With me speeding down, the roll of the ship increased the pull of gravity. To tell you the truth, gravity didn't give a fuck about me anyway. I bounced as I hit the deck. The LCP was rising up, and with all that energy, I was airborne. While I was in flight, I was thinking that if the flamethrower had napalm plus gas, I would have sunk the troop ship. Someone said, "Castello is hurt."

Gunny yelled, "Go back and find out if he's hurt. If not, I'll hurt him."

The coxswain sent the LCP onto the beach and dropped the ramp, and we charged, firing blanks. This was the first time but not the last time that it was the United States versus Michael Castello. Gunny was running wild on the beach. He had his bayonet stuck to his rifle and was screaming, "Kill them fucking gooks." I saw a gook once, and he didn't look much different than me.

Climbing the hill was tough until I saw a young gook, smaller than me, carrying an icebox on his back and selling Coca Cola. This is the kind of enemy I like. Instead of firing bullets, he was firing sandwiches and Coca Colas. We captured the high ground and secured the area. The day passed into night. The moon was shining. I never saw a more beautiful sight, except when I saw flashes of that flaming pussy at the gas station.

A couple of days later, all of us were on liberty, and a few of us ended up in a bar that had all the earmarks of a slaughterhouse. The place was full of marines and sailors. The ladies of the night were watched closely by pimps, who saw that no harm came to the ladies. We warmed up with rum and with a good dose of piss. The girls were busy getting their pussies sucked. The ladies sat on the bar with their legs wide open. They charged one dollar for thirty seconds and extra dollar for a splash of rum on her pussy. Business started picking up.

There were three lines. The middle line was the piggyback. At no extra charge, the ladies grabbed a head of hair, jammed your face into their snatch, and as it was getting good, they pushed your head down and grabbed the hair of the guy on top and shoved his face into her snatch. That was the good news. The bad news was when I jumped onto the bar and started singing the Marine Corps hymn. The sailors started singing "Anchors Away." The bartender was livid with rage, and he was yelling for me to get off the bar. I started kicking shot glasses at him, and he went down and then came up with a machete and ran toward me. The troops started throwing bottles at the fuck. The window busted, and guys were jumping out. I caught a foot from the lady of the night. I made it out with the bitch on my back, ripping the hair off of my head. I was done!

The cops arrested me, and all I remember was that I was placed in a dungeon below ground. The night air knocked me out cold. The next morning I was taken to the ship and was diagnosed as being poisoned.

I was ready to sue Puerto Rico. The captain saw me in the brig with restraining belts. He looked at me and said, "One day a hero, the next day a wrecking machine."

When the black ocean was covered with phosphorus, it made the ocean look like a god that all men and women would want to believe in. If I had jumped into that ocean, I would have avoided a life of paranoia, and to make matters worse, being ultra-short. That was hard to deal with. I settled for jerking off into the ocean, and that was the best piece of ass I ever had.

The return trip back was a religious experience. The rising sun breaking the horizon, the flying fish, the rain, and the ocean were a tribute to Mother Nature. A young man who thought he had all the answers was about to find out that his report card began and ended with zero. My entire life revolved around action. We arrived at Morehead City, and back at base things were the same. The quanson huts, the second front, were a strip of bloody buckets. The women, with the sweet smell of pussy, reinvigorated me.

I became the driver of an amphibian truck. We transported ammunition, supplies, and troops, and we had to know every aspect of the truck. I drove blind at night with only a dim red light to follow. The truck in front of me was racing at breakneck speed while carrying cans of gas and live ammunition. There was a fog of red dust. Danger was there, but so was excitement, and the excitement was like sex.

I took a few guys out for a spin, and we patrolled the river. I took out the floorboards, tied them to the line, and let out twenty feet. Two guys hopped into the water, balls-ass naked. We took off. People who lived on the river called in that there was a boatload of marines out of uniform. Base was notified, and they sent out a patrol boat. We figured that someone would call and put the patrol boat on us.

We could see quite a distance on the river, and we decided to evade the patrol boat by going through an area that was conducting rifle fire. We approached the area, and the trees were riddled with rifle fire. In the dead zone, we could see and hear the rifle fire and the bullets striking the water. As soon as the rifle fire stopped, we took off and made a run for it. I said, "You got to go when you got to go." We got back by outmaneuvering the patrol boat. The captain called me in and asked me about it. I said that I took the boat on shore to check a valve that was blowing air. He said, "You got me," but added, "Don't do it anymore, doing what you didn't do."

I had some liberty time and rounded up some guys who were interested in taking a ride to New York City. I got a few volunteers, and we all had enough money. I told them we'd be staying at my mom's house. They were hot to trot. I figured that if we all chipped in for gas, we could end up having a good time. In 1946, people were driving cars that were made in the early thirties. The car I had was a Nash, and it could move. I could do a hundred plus on the road. We left on Friday at four on the main highway, which was 301, a winding two-lane road through the woods. There was no I-95, just a killer road. I was a good driver, and I was trying to make time before it got dark.

Somewhere in Virginia, we came upon an accident. We slowed down and stopped to see what took place. The site was horrible. There were three people in a car that was burning. It seemed like they were sitting there in a calm manner, and I was praying they were not marines. Any person in his right mind who would not pay attention to the danger that we were surrounded by had to be callous. Dismissing the scene rendered me insane. We moved on, and later we came upon a tractor that was burning. The driver behind the wheel was fighting for his life. We saw pure white flames with a black silhouette of a human, doing the dance of death.

I took the wheel and drove sixty miles an hour for twenty minutes, and then my speed was up to eighty. We were moving on. I was behind a tractor for a number of miles and was hoping to get a shot to pass him. I pulled out and opened it up. The driver saw I was alongside of him. He waited until I was up to his door, and he was matching my speed. I looked at his face, and a chill ran up my spine. I thought I was looking at the devil!

A truck was coming into view, and the marine alongside of me was frozen with fear. I had my foot to the floor. I had no choice; I had to press on. I never took my eyes off the truck that was coming on strong. I had ten seconds left, and I turned into the truck alongside of me, thinking I was going to hit. He braked at the last second and let me through. Both drivers blasted their horns. The electricity from the horns ran through my body. As I slowed down, they were still blasting away, and that was a momentous point in my life. Did I learn anything? No. Did I give a fuck about anything? No. God have mercy on someone else's soul.

The marine next to me screamed, "Stop!" I pulled over and looked at his face. It was contorted, and he was crying. He then opened the door of the car. I asked if anyone wanted to get out, and no one answered my call.

We were in Virginia, and it was hot. I took my clothes off and was completely in the nude. The only thing I had on were my shoes as we moved through the city. I was exceeding the speed limit and was coming to an intersection. A dump truck was crossing my lane to make a left turn, and I was doing fifty in a twenty-five-mile-per-hour zone. I was timing the truck. I knew that I would make it and never slowed down.

I swerved around the truck, not knowing that a state trooper was watching the whole episode. He rolled alongside of me and motioned for me to pull over. He got out of his car, walked over to me, and said, "I was sure you would hit that truck." I told him I had room to spare. He asked to see my license. I grabbed a pile of clothes I was sitting on and rummaged through them. I found my wallet and pulled out snapshots of a whore getting fucked along with my license. He said, "This is no license. This is a boat license." He looked at me and said, "Are you planning on taking a shower? You idiot, you almost killed yourself and three other men."

Then he said, "I know you're a marine, and I understand the need for pussy to live. So watch the way you drive. I am going to make a list of all your violations." The list had fifteen violations on it. He let me go but told me not to come back through this area. The three marines riding with me were betting on who would be alive when we got back to base.

We arrived in Brooklyn. My mom cooked a dinner, and then we went to Coney Island. We had fun on the rides and then headed back to base.

I was about to get out, but I wanted to pay a visit to Mom Tiny's place. I had waited a month to get five days off, and when Mom Tiny saw me come through the door, she had that skunk-eating shit smile on her face, and I had a pussy-eating smile on my face. I picked out my favorite whore and wanted to fall in love with her.

We went for walks, and she was very interesting. She told me about her love life, and that gave me a nightmare. The thought of her with a hundred sawed-off cocks in her mouth was too freakish to contemplate.

My love life diminished to the point that the word love became a dirty word. I was released from the marines and returned to New York City. I moved into Mom and Dad's place. Since I had some experience in cutting hair, I thought that maybe I could become a beautician, until some clown told me that only gays were beauticians.

I was looking at hairstyles, and every other style was different and challenging. The only proof the guy who told me all beauticians were gay was right was that my dad had a customer who was a beautician, and he was gay. Because of that, my life was thrust into the path of a locomotive. Instead of taking the A train, I took the zero train.

I took good old Dad's advice and applied to a barber school. My teacher was a scumbag from the old school. Our customers were New York City's finest. The Bowery bums, although many were once judges and doctors, were now skid-row bums. There was no protection for these individuals; they were beaten on the soles of their feet to awaken them. I can't imagine any pain worse than that. Skid row was full of hate. The barber school was a place where you could commit homicide on a head. I had to stop the bleeding, stitch a gash with a safety pin, and then steam clean my customer's face to see if he was related to me. Thank God he was in a state of semideath. Hot steam on an open sore returned him to life.

One of my associates, a kid of fifteen years, was working in a chair next to me. His father was a well-known, made man who drove and picked his son up each day. He spotted me and asked if I was Italian. I spoke a few words in Italian, and he told me I was responsible for his son. I told him his son would return to him a wiser man. You had to talk to these guys half in Italian and half in Chinese.

One day an individual walked in on his own volition. He was a tall, dark, and handsome man with long black hair. He said, "It took years to grow to that point." He spoke with a cadence that was hard to understand, and it took good judgment on my part to unravel what he really wanted. He gave me the justification to use my own discretion, which was lacking at times. I called my associate and explained what the gentleman wanted. I explained that we needed to run the clipper very quickly along the side of his head. The machine was shaking in my associate's hand, and as he thrust the clipper, it got stuck in the client's hair. I noticed every sinew in the stranger's head. His reaction was to leap out of the chair. The clipper was yanked out of the socket. He fled out of the shop with the clipper clinging to the side of his head.

The boy looked at me and said, "My clipper!"

I said, "That's a lesson you must learn. People will do anything to steal something."

In the old days, when gays were less appreciated, we had a customer called Queenie who looked like he had received many blow jobs on his head. He glided into the chair. He bounced around like he was having an orgasm. He needed a facial, a shave, and a shampoo. I lowered the chair over the sink and scrubbed his head with a toilet brush as my associate watched every move. The shave came next. I lathered his face until every discernible feature was covered with lather. I applied the towel that was steaming hot and held the two ends of the towel, imprisoning him momentarily. I made sure that the steam was penetrating deeply. He fought to get out of the chair. Then he broke loose and ran for the door.

The instructor was very cognizant of my attributes as a barber. He told me that if I made one more move like that, I would be doughnut shit. When I left the school for the day, I went to the barbershop. Customers from the local schools came for haircuts, and my job was to get the ball rolling. I put the board on the seat and the paper around the boy's neck, and then I wrapped the cloth around him. Dad showed me how to use the clipper. I then turned the kid over to him and watched. I would do one step at a time until I was ready to finish the job. In a way, a kid is the same as any man. My father was a good barber, and I tried to be better. After a while, I was given a kid to do. Once I got the hang of it, I styled the kids' hair. Their mothers complained that their children looked like gangsters. They wanted their kids to look like kids, not like pimps. I pasted whiskers on them.

The word was out, and the hoods started coming around. Most of the mothers were Jewish, and at times they thought we were being held up. They got over it fast when the high rollers paid the moms for the seat. The sidewalk was wide, and the neighborhood mothers parked their carriages, looking for a spot in the sun. The hoods were eyeballing the kids, and one yelled, "All these fucking kids look like Mike."

One guy who owned a gas station—the same gas station I worked in when I was a kid—came by. He was out of the pen a few months before we hit it off. The barber shop had a room that was six by six, and it had shelves. Some customers had their own tools, while others decided to bring their own boxes. I made sure they had locks on the boxes. I did not want my dad to think that I had an armory. The room was used for quick blow jobs. The barber chair was great, and the girls got real freaky when they walked into the back room. Seeing the chair really got them hot.

There was one woman who was a French war bride, and she was the hottest of the hot. She was able to wrap her tongue around an ice cream cone. It was pure sex, and once she drove me to the back room to jerk off. I took three strokes and popped. I stepped out of the back room, and my cock was manageable. I had to get rid of her kid. No matter where I stood in the shop, my cock was always pointing at her.

There was a new type of haircut that was the rage. I took a look at it. It was simple enough, and the kids loved it. They were lining up. The kids in the carriages were screaming to suck a tit. In the meantime, a few of the moms who had boyfriends picked them up for a quick afternoon delight. They had me babysitting. The women had boyfriends who had money, and in the long run, everyone was happy. I think I started the first dating game.

My dad had smiles up the ass. He had a license to do rubdowns, and he worked them over good. He had his customers moaning in the chair. The mirror on the wall was huge. The barber chair was God's gift to man. You could crank a woman upside down if you wanted to. That chair gave you the ability to display every crevice in a woman's body. One woman was so hot. She rolled over onto her belly, and that drove me to the back room. I had a small business on the side because that I was in the bowery. The stores armed the average thief. They had every device. They could set you up to start your own thievery business. Some wanted to change their looks so they would not to be identified. I went from shop to shop buying handcuffs, mustaches, beards, dildos wrapped in sandpaper, marked cards, and loaded dice. You might say, "Forget about it," but the human being is so complex that a super salesman could sell a bag of shit if he knew what buttons to press.

One clown walked into the barbershop one day looking for a flat top. He pulled off a score two blocks from where he lived. I asked why he didn't wear a hat, and he said he didn't want to mess up his hair. The hoodlum from the gas station started coming around. When I closed the shop, I stopped by the gas station to shoot the shit about crime and pussy. At that time, pussy and crime were the nicest words in the dictionary. John had a brother who was a legit guy to a point, the only legit job in America was being a barber. I had to bust my balls for every fucking nickel I made. That's what I hated the most. Every morning I had to come in and do the same thing over and over again.

John, with his forked tongue, ran a story about him and his partner rounding up people waiting to deposit money in the bank and then rolling away in a car that had a slab of steel across the backseat to stop gunshots from coming through. John looked like the movie actor Joseph Cotton. He was around five-ten and had a slim build. He wanted to know if I wanted a broad who was living in his pad with his girlfriend. The girl was released from the House of Good Shepherds, a reformatory. John told me she had fucked every doorknob in the house, and the poor bastard had to wash his hands every time he opened the door.

I knew she was for me. John took over the stage and was rapping about the joint. I really dug the broad. She was in her teens, with red hair, and was hot to fuck. After a few beers, John and Nancy made no move to leave. The room was a stage. The kitchen was wide open, and the bed was a cot with squeaky springs. John and Nancy were taken in the scene, and Ginger was hot to trot. I took her with her clothes on. I pulled her panties aside, entered her, and immediately popped. Three minutes later, I popped again. I was able to maintain an erection for as long as I wanted. The squeaky springs were music to my ears.

John was fucking Nancy on the table. She was screaming, Ginger was moaning, the dog was fucking the cat, and the rats were eating the cheese. The Lord said, "Why eat bread when the woman wants to give you head?" We continued fucking. Her pussy was the color of a fire raging. Between the fucking and the sucking, I jerked off to get my prick to surrender. John said, "Rosa is getting out of jail in a couple of weeks. Check her out. I'm sure she will give you a ride that you will never forget."

Two weeks went by, and I was pussy whipped. I took off for eight hours to let my balls rest. With two weeks in a steam pipe, my nuts needed to be coddled. On the day Rosa got out, John asked me if I wanted Rosa or Ginger. I had a way of knowing what I wanted. I had no pad, and Rosa was moving in and Ginger was moving out. John said Rosa was insane. He fucked her in a church confessional. He said he almost killed her to keep the noise down. I told him that's what I wanted—the hunchback back of Notre Dame. The secret of an ugly woman's fantasy is deceptive to the point of insanity. If you jab your finger up her asshole, she will jump ten feet. I really don't want to quote God on this one. *Write me a letter if you don't understand some bullshit thing I wrote!*

John called Lucky, and the kid showed up. John asked Lucky if he wanted Ginger, and Lucky said yeah. Ginger looked at him and said, "I love you, Lucky." He was extremely handsome. He had light hair, was five-foot-six, had a good shape, and looked like James Dean. We hit it off. He got the girl with the flaming pussy, and I got the hunchback. Nevertheless, Rosa was burning. She had a broken nose, bow legs, kinky hair, broken teeth, sixty pounds of pure muscle, and ghostly skin. She was fearless and provocative and loved combat. She demanded brutality, and she dished it out.

Rosa came home spotted me. "Where's Lucky?" she asked.

John said, "He took off for a couple of weeks."

Her snatch had a little hair, her crack was three inches long, and she had the smallest pussy I ever saw. She sucked the foreskin off the head of my cock, and foreplay was ripping the skin off my back. The more she brutalized me, the hotter I got. She denied me entry, and my cock was losing respect. I took a dive, and her three-inch crack opened. I ran my head so deep that I was looking out of her asshole. I drove my tongue into her and chewed away, and the harder I chewed, the more she turned into a devil. God whispered into my ear, "This is the closest you will ever get to heaven."

She was so hot. When we came together, it was like riding a bronco. Our movements were strong, and I knew this woman was for me. I also knew I had to hurt a few guys to keep her under control. I dried up the field, and they soon found out I was too dangerous to fuck with. No matter what, I found an equalizer.

I still had to go to work each day. Rosa was on the loose, and it was a cat and mouse game. At night we fucked like animals. When I thought I was hurting her too much, she would look at me, smile, and then up the ante. I knew the direction I was headed for—destruction. I was hooked, and I had the devil for a partner. I loved her every move, and she turned me on. I was ashamed of her looks, and that dichotomy drove me crazy.

I loved my mother, and each day as I passed her house to go to work, she would be at the window. I wished she would die so I would not feel guilty. That made me angry. Rosa's brother got in a fight with a couple of guys, and they broke a cement block over his head. John was in charge of the plan to get the guys. He was on the phone talking and then blurted out, "Charlie Irish is coming down with some of his boys to lend a hand."

I asked, "Who's this guy?"

John lowered his voice in deference, trying to conjure up the right words to say. "You'll see when he gets here."

Time passed by. John kept the gas station open. At 2:00 a.m., four cars circled the station. One guy jumped out, checked out a few cars on the lot, and then went into the garage. He kicked the dog in the ass for growling at him. "Who's the owner of this flea-infested barrel of used oil?" he asked.

John raised his hand, and the hood patted him down. He told the rest of us to keep our hands where he could see them. He pulled out a zip gun and waved the okay sign, and Charlie Irish stepped out of the car. Then four cars in unison opened their doors, and they stepped out. One guy stepped out and tripped. Charlie Irish, like a flash, kicked him in the ribs and started screaming, "The war hasn't been declared yet, and you went down without a shot!" Then he gave him three more kicks in the ribs. I said to myself, *This has to be staged.*

Charlie Irish walked over to John with a noticeable limp. His height was five-foot-eight. He was muscular and an incarnation of James Cagney. He was wearing a green cardigan jacket and red peg pants. A chain ran from his wallet down to his ankles and up to his belt. His hat had a brim that blocked out the light from his face. He wore sunglasses and had spit-shined shoes, and when he opened his mouth, every word was concise. "How do we destroy these people?" he asked. He went into a tirade and took over the gas station. He told the guy with the bruised ribs to fill the tanks and check the oil.

He cleaned out the desk and started to formulate a battle plan to raise a couple of hundred men. "Before we take care of those two guys," he said, and I'll never forget his next words, "we must punish Canarsie."

John wanted to close up before the boys cleaned out the garage. Charlie Irish was walking around, pointing at things to throw into the car. He wanted to take the dog and leave the guy who kicked the dog in the ass. John said, "The dog has fleas."

I took a liking to Charlie Irish. With him there never could be a dull moment. We arranged a meeting for the next day. We went to Coney Island, and he introduced me to guys who were sticking up guys for gas money. Charlie Irish wanted a pledge from the leader of each gang! And he came on strong, saying as he pulled out a revolver, "This represents ninety people!" The words were released from his mouth quick. Anyone who questioned him was confronted with a gun to his head. He laid out a plan: "I need trucks to carry troops, weapons, and rocks to break windows on Main Street and to set fire to cars. We'll put on hoods to disguise ourselves." As dumb as I was, I knew this guy was a comedian

I played around with him. He was funny! The next day he never mentioned anything about Canarsie. He had balls; there was a lot of fun in Brooklyn. The rumors were alive, and word spread from one neighborhood to another all night long, pouring gasoline on stories. This guy was a stool pigeon, that guy busted into a club. Charlie Irish was the Goebbels of Brooklyn and conned guys into getting into the car. I was the driver. He started accusing them of something or another, and I put the rearview mirror on the guy's face. I saw the bulging eyeballs and heard the no's as an invalid voice pleaded for mercy. Out came the four-way lug wrench. There was bang on the fucking head, the screams of a banshee, bang again, and blood running. The door would open, and Charlie Irish's gimp leg would hold him back. He would swing and miss.

Charlie Irish was strong, and with one shot, he could take your head off. He was a master with the four-way lug wrench. He used it as a tuning fork. He had control. He could maim you or tame you. The guy was an actor and could have been somebody. To tell you the truth, he was somebody. Charlie Irish took me to his home, and I met his wife for the first time. I never met a woman like her. She was all curves and wore high heels and a miniskirt. In the forties, they had skirts down to the knees. She had a body that could stop a clock. She opened the refrigerator door, bent over to get a beer, and a shock wave went through my brain. After seeing the crack of her ass, I had to turn around to see if a cowboy had a branding iron in my brain.

Charlie Irish screamed, "Where's the fucking food?"

She screamed back, "The pork chops were growing a fur coat, and by the way, who's that clown with you?"

Charlie Irish stuck his chest out and said, "That's the negotiator. He stopped a war in Canarsie."

I told her that I cut hair. She asked if I cut women's hair. I said I cut a few styles. The way she sat on the couch made my tongue stiff. I was lost for words; I was mesmerized. I went for a beer, took a long swig, and told Charlie Irish, "Your wife is driving me nuts." He laughed, and we all laughed after that. I talked to her in any fucking way I could. She knew I respected her husband, and I respected her.

Charlie Irish wanted me to meet a crew on Broadway. They were mugging tourists or anyone who looked soft. There were eight of them, and if they scored for seven bucks, there could be a shootout. I told Charlie Irish, "This is no good. We need to knock off a few scores." I ran it down to the guys, and four backed down. The new crew was Charlie Irish, Black Nicky, Jerry the Jew, me, and Broadway Louie. I stole the cars and was the driver. Our base was Forty-Sixth and Broadway. We went to Sunnyside, Greenpoint, and Ridgewood, cruising around and looking for a score.

I spotted a joint and pulled over, and Charlie Irish and the boys went in. I waited so long that the dial was sitting on E. I decided to go in. Charlie Irish was pacing around, and I said, "What's the problem?"

He said, "He's got a two foot cleaver in his hand!" I yanked the gun from his belt, went behind the counter, and told the guy to get in the back room. He dropped the cleaver and seemed relieved that the waiting was all over. Jerry the Jew tied the guy with his own tie, and Charlie Irish cleaned out the register and then took two dozen bialys and ten pounds of lox for his wife. We went out the door and back to Broadway.

Our hangout was a bar. We were acting like the Jesse James boys. Charlie Irish bragged to the prostitute that I was lightning. He was buying drinks. I was in my glory. I had a few drinks, a bag of chips, and fifty bucks for my cut. As I drove back to East New York, I was happy about the heist. I knew I had the power. I gave the orders when it came to the scores. Charlie Irish was a gang leader, not a heist man. My interest was in capturing the interest of those being robbed.

I was happy that Charlie's wife got the biggest cut. I parked the car and then changed the plate back to the original car. The owner of the car lived in the neighborhood, and before he left for work, I cut his engine wire. When I got back, I spliced the wire. What bugged me was that it cost me two bucks for gas.

I jumped into the car, picked up Rosa, and headed for the club. I loved dancing with Rosa, and I made her take her panties off. While we danced, I lifted up her dress to see her bowlegs and that tight ass. It turned the joint wild. Rosa was happy, and I was happy. I couldn't wait until I tore her pussy up.

A couple of days later, we dumped Black Nicky. He was on dope, and being a dope is no good. We hit a gas station. The owner hid the money in his pants but left a few bucks in the register. I shook him down for a gun, because I read in the papers that one owner killed a heist man. I didn't find a gun, but I found a stash of $2,500. I thought I was going to die. Charlie Irish's wife gave me a kiss, plus a foot of tongue. I had enough money to buy a Ford convertible with a red interior.

Charlie Irish got busted for a minor charge, and the gang broke up. I headed back to the gas station. I hooked up with John, Lucky, and Ralph. The gang was going for payrolls. I loved the detective aspect of it—watching, following, disguises. We averaged ten grand a hit and split it four ways. I had a lot of money to spend at the clubs. Rosa dyed her hair dark red. Her pussy hairs drove me nuts until someone told me that the hair in my nose was on fire.

I did a transaction with John over a couple of guns. He had a guy who sold guns from the trunk of his car. John picked some up for peanuts and charged me a hundred apiece. I was showing a fellow thief the guns, and he asked what I paid for them. I said, "A hundred dollars each." I asked,

"What did you pay?" and he said half. I was so fucking mad. I was putting my life on the line with him, and he gave an outsider a better deal.

I got a hold of John and told him the story. I knew I was done with him. I loved Rosa, but there was no way I could shack up with her. The last thing I needed was a ball and chain. Lucky wanted me to forget the argument. I said that I had no confidence in John anymore. A week later Lucky was killed, and John and Ralph were shot.

Rosa and I went to the wake. She was dressed in black. I looked at her hat. It was too small, her dress was too big, and she had one heel that was shorter than the other. As she walked to the coffin, she was crying, and I knew she loved Lucky. He was gentle with her. I had a feeling that if I was in that box, she would be cracking a bottle of booze. She was so unusual, so outstanding, so different, and so variable. But most of all, she was desirable.

Lucky, John, and Ralph, according to the newspaper, had entered a club in the Village, and after hanging around, they pulled guns and shots were fired. People dove for cover. One guy went to call the cops. The crew decided to take off and ran into a guy who went for the cops. They shot him in the head, but he survived. A cop, hearing gunshots, went toward the sound of gunfire and ran into the crew as they got into the car for the getaway. The officer opened fire and shot two men. Lucky ran, and two detectives followed him into a basement club. They shot Lucky to death.

The Korean War started, and this was my chance to break away from a lifestyle that inevitably would lead to my death. The gangster life was zero. My chances were better with the marines, where the death rate was 90 percent. I wanted action. I had a death wish. The assault platoon would honor my wish. I would remember the times Rosa and I hit the clubs and started having a good time. She would say something that pushed my buttons, or I would talk to some woman she didn't like. That sealed the night for retaliation. We would leave the club, not saying a word, get in the car, and drive slowly away, as if it were our last drive.

John was in jail, and Nancy was seeing her ex-lover. A trip to her house took us to an elevated line that was connected to the subway. It was a mile run on a narrow two-lane road that ran between the posts that held up the train tracks. There was a service road on the outside of the post. As we entered, I looked ahead, and it appeared like a solid steel pipe. I was doing ten miles an hour. I glanced at Rosa, and she was smiling. I looked ahead as cars were crossing the intersections. I was up to twenty mph, and at that speed, the intersections were coming up fast. I looked at her, and she was still smiling. I had to brake to keep from killing a carload of people. She laughed out loud as I pushed the car to fifty. The end of the tunnel was coming up, and a car was coming into the intersection. I had no time to stop. I switched lanes as a man, frozen with fear, let me through. I wiped the smile off her face.

I parked the car, and she ripped my pants to get at my cock. She inflicted pain. We were in love again! To sustain a lust so incendiary, one must forfeit his life. I made a life-or-death decision and told Rosa I had lost interest in her. She said, "Fuck you," and that was the last time I saw her.

I went to the recruiting office to get back into the marines. I was accepted and was told I had less than a month before they called me. I met a lot of buddies the second time around. It was no joke. The men were older and had families. I was the same guy with an edge, robbing people with a gun, and street fighting. It was a form of combat. I could afford to throw my life away because I had no concept of what life could be. I got my education by associating with people who had no regard for anyone or anything. I wanted to get into their minds, to protect myself from the day when a murderer might want to kill me.

I listened to friends talk about things that were so dangerous that I was able to put a timeline on their lives. I had many friends who had the need to say things out loud when they were putting a guy down and forfeit their lives. To warn someone not to say this or that is only prolonging the death sentence. The criminal mind wants you to be careful. It will turn to paranoia when you put yourself in danger.

What I did the second time around was no different than the first time. The only thing different was that we were at war. I was sure I would go to Korea. I wanted to have a license to kill. It had nothing to do with patriotism. I loved my country, and I would die for America. I knew we would win the war. The thing was, I really wanted to shoot some poor bastard in the head. I spoke to my company commander and asked him to send me to Korea. I was told that we had to train, and we did train. I asked to be transferred to tanks, but we never were called.

The prostitutes kept me busy. There was nothing like worn-out pussy. I had a buddy from Ashland, Kentucky, whose father was a preacher. My buddy was stone crazy. He talked me into going AWOL with him and heading for Kentucky. There were three of us. One was a tough Polish marine who could clean out a bar full of sailors. He was in my outfit.

We took off in October. I had my uniform, an overcoat, gloves, and thirty dollars. It was a cold day. The plan was to hitch a ride to Kentucky. We stood on the side of the road till our balls were falling off. I was holding onto mine to keep my hands warm. My balls turned to acorns.

We walked for hours, and finally some drunk came along and said he would take us a couple of hundred miles. We talked him into letting one of us drive. He passed out, and we went an extra hundred miles and then stopped at a diner. He was still out, it was almost dawn, and the weather was getting colder. As we got close to a small town, we started knocking on doors to get warm, and finally someone came to the door. It took him ten minutes to cross the floor, and then he opened the door to let us in. The old man was sitting in a chair. He pulled himself across the floor. He had a potbelly stove, and the warmth crept into my bones. The man was afraid, and I tried to ease his fear. One hour later we left and thanked him.

We came to a bus station, and our buddy slipped out on us there. We were thirty miles from Ashland, Kentucky, and down to a few bucks each. I knew the kid's last name and got a phone book. There must have been twenty names the same as his. The first person I called was his cousin, and I told her we were in the marines together. She gave me his phone number. I called, and he came to pick us up and take us to his home.

His mother and her preacher husband looked at me as if I were a monkey in a cage. We got around to talking about what kind of Christian I was. I told them I was Catholic. They had a devil in the house, and they could ask the devil questions. They asked about the pope and were surprised when I didn't know his name. I had to describe the church, the saints, the nuns, and how the nuns kneeled on the sidewalk and begged for money for the poor. They were surprised.

Once I met a southern girl at a barn dance. She was young and beautiful. I flipped over this special beauty, and we danced and talked. She had a tough time understanding me and thought I was a foreigner. I spoke

Brooklynese. I had a tough time understanding her southern accent, but I made her laugh. She was becoming interested in me. She asked me what my denomination was. I thought she wanted to know if I was a five-, ten-, or twenty-dollar bill. Before I could answer, she asked what my religion was. I said, "Catholic," and she said, "I can't talk to you," and turned and walked away.

I was trying to show the preacher and his wife that Catholics were good people. His son was a screwball, and the father seemed bewildered by him. He asked his father for the keys to his car. We went to bars, and his son got very drunk and was hard to handle. We had a hit and run, and in the morning, his father saw the damage. I was ashamed. I told Ski it was time to go. The son wanted to show us a road that ran along the side of a mountain called Suicide Run. It ran from the top of the mountain into town. The road was icy and winding all the way. We got to the top, spun around, and headed back down. The car had no seatbelts, and no safety glass. He knew how to handle the wheel but not the ice. On the way down, he flipped the car a number of times and ended up on the wheels. I'm sure I had a concussion, and I had knots all over my head. I seemed to get the worst of it.

We got back into the car and went to the dance. I had an ice bag on my head. The next day I felt okay. The kid wanted to stay, and his mother wanted to give us money. Ski and I said no, and the kid drove us to the highway.

This time we stopped at a bus station to get some sleep and started hiking by day. It was easier with just the two of us. We arrived at Quantico and turned ourselves in. We had to face some serious charges, and I had to come up with a story. I went before the captain and explained that I met a lady at a dance who was married. I told him we fell in love. She told me she wanted to divorce her husband and marry me. The officer who was taking notes started laughing and could not stop. I said, "Ski was my best man."

The captain told the officer to stop laughing. I had the guy rolling. I added that she needed three hundred dollars to pay for the divorce but I only had two hundred. There was more laughter. I gave her the money and she took it, saying she would come down when she got the papers. The captain said to me, "You sack of shit."

There was more laughter, and then the officer said, "Give them a break." I received a deck court martial, the lowest form of court martial. We were back in the brig for ten days with just bread and water. We spent the time telling fuck stories. I got real good at bringing out the hottest details. I knew the story was hot because of the stiffness of my cock. One inmate told how he met his wife and gave every detail. Some would ask, "Did you do it this way or that way?" The fucking guards would listen to the stories.

I was impressed with the power of sex on the human mind, especially an eighteen-year-old. I should've taken advantage of the power sex had on people. The actual act, once performed a number of times, diminishes, if a man's partner is the same person, no matter how beautiful she is. The sex-driven machine needs to fantasize to keep its drive going. A business in erotic sex, from the lowest to the highest level, could be very profitable.

The war was slowing down. I was put on every shit detail that came along. KP was the worst. The field kitchen duty was out in the woods, boiling water to clean trays that they dumped, food and all. I had to get a blow torch to pry them open. The marines turned me into a nonredeemable asshole.

My time was up. I wanted a shortcut to riches, and I received a shortcut to nowhere. I was back on the corner, and no one even knew I was gone. One guy said, "Where the fuck was you?" Could I tell him that I was fighting for America?

I went to the corner looking for Charlie. He was working for his dad and was married to a girl named Margie. He fixed me up with a girl named Alice. Alice's family was Sicilian, and they taught their daughter that men were Satan. Alice and I hit it off quick; she was seventeen and a virgin. She had tits that were like rocks. Her mother knew Margie and liked her. School was out, and she allowed Alice to hang around Margie's house. I took over and drove her around Ridgewood, near her house.

I knew a gang in the area, hit a few places, and introduced her to the boys. She took to the action and loved the clubs. They were designed by a wino. I knew that foreplay was to addict her to the free spirit of the unemployed. Every article in most clubs was stolen. The furniture was stolen from the vestibules of high rises. Dildos, toilet seats, and scumbags hung from the ceiling, and on the wall was a crucifix. The rumor was that if you touched the cross, the heat from sin would burn your hand.

She was spellbound. She was raised from childhood that sinning would cause her to be struck by lightning; she didn't realize that she would be holding the hand of Satan. I chased a few guys from the club; modesty was paramount.

At this stage of the game, I applied all the things Mom Tiny taught me. I worked her without penetration. I sucked her virgin pussy and opened the flood gates to a wonderful start. I held off from taking her virginity. I wanted her to make that call. I liked her, but I had no lust for her. I doubt if I will ever love anyone. I was lustful! The opiate of sex was all consuming; it consumed love, fidelity, and the Ten Commandments. She was pleased that she still had her virginity, but in the heat of the moment, she begged me to fuck her. I gave her time to understand that my life was a selfish one. Can anyone whose loins are on fire promise anyone that he would forever love? Nonsense.

Margie called me up and said, "Do me a favor. Come over and fuck this girl." Penetration day became Independence Day. I liberated every hole in her body. Our love life became superficial, with a quick blow job and a promise of fidelity! I made up the most outlandish lies. My mind was preoccupied with coming up with a score.

Willie Sutton was a hero to me, and his motto was: banks are where the money is. I sat alone in a car casing guys coming to banks with money bags. You can tell the type of work they do just by the way they dressed. The guy had a sign on his apron or his shirt with a local supermarket. Most parked in the same spot every time, and that gave me an edge. When it was time to take the money to the bank, he made a beeline to the car, opened the door, and jumped in, in a great hurry to get back to work. He was not paying attention to what was going on.

A week later, I struck as he opened the door to get into his car. I grabbed his hair and jammed the barrel of the gun hard into his ribs. I cuffed him to the brake pedal, took his bag, and left. I tried not to talk to him. On the right day, you can get a year's wages. I was showing Charlie the score, and he was ready to shoot his father to get out of the factory. With the money, I got clothes and bought a newer car.

Alice was trapped in her house, and that elevated her need to see me. Being hot was one thing, but being seventeen made her much hotter for me. When I stopped coming around, the family sent her to the old country. It's a culture that should be embraced. After reading a book over a dozen times, you should return it to the library. Charlie wanted me to put him down on my next score, but I was in no hurry to move that quick. I was back on the corner and started hanging around. The name of the game was to fuck around.

People were coming down from the elevated line and stopping in for coffee. Sometimes we would fuck with them. One black guy decided not to take any shit, and we were face to face. He saw that he was outnumbered and gave us the finger as he walked out the door. I picked up a sugar bowl and threw it at him. He took off. Two detectives from the Seventy-Fifth Precinct were riding by, and seeing some action, they grabbed me. I put up a fight, and the black, seeing what was going on, came back and told the detectives I threw a sugar bowl at him. I was arrested and taken to the precinct, where they worked me over for a while, saying, "You want to fight cops!" I had cuffs on. They hoisted me up, and I was hanging by my wrists. They asked if I was going to complain like a pussy. I said, "You'll get no beef out of me." I swung for a while. I was charged with assault and spent the night in jail.

At the court house I was given bond and went before a judge. While I was waiting to be called up, I looked at the black man, who was dressed in uniform, and I really felt bad. I was called to the bench asked if I was guilty or not. I pleaded guilty. I had no lawyer, and the judge gave me one year of probation. He also said, "This is how it starts. You are a wolf in sheep's clothing. First assault, then burglary, then robbery, and then you end up in the electric chair."

My mother was sitting in court, and she said, "Mike, I have a burning feeling in my chest." I stared into her eyes, and I knew I had hurt her. As much as I loved her, I knew I would continue to hurt her. The probation officer told me to find a job or go to jail, and so I went back to the barbershop. I needed time to think. The shop was a place I could use and still rob and make a decent living. The boys came around, and the ladies still were sucking cock like they were lollipops. The hoods still came around, and one of my younger sister's friends would pass the shop. I got to hang out with her, and we became lovers. She was the youngest of ten kids. Her father and mother were the finest people I had ever met.

The neighborhood, with the old homes, the sand dunes, the swamp, and the farms, was bought by the city of New York. We were given time to leave our homes. The process had started years before. The guys were getting married, and I really wanted to get married to see what the bullshit was about. I asked my lady to marry me, and we took off for Maryland to get married. Her dad was heartbroken, and being the fuck that I was, I never considered anybody else's feelings. I had fresh pussy, and she seemed to enjoy it. Satiation should never be fulfilled. A human must be hungry for lust and revenge.

My wife was a happy person until she married me. The only thing we had in common was that we loved to fuck. My father had a four-family house on Hageman Avenue. I took over the apartments and was the only one living there. My father bought a four-family home next door to the barbershop, and the family moved in. Then all hell broke loose. That's all I can say. I don't want a hit man following me around.

The Jews started blowing town, and most left for greener pastures. The Italians held on in the hope that the projects were going to be full of Polacks. Much to their dismay, a boom box woke them up. The apartment was okay, and I and my wife moved in. We were told that we had to move out soon; they let us stay till the last. I paid twenty dollars a month, and we used what was left of the furniture. It was good enough. We had heat from an oil burner. I had a couple of guns. There were a number of people who didn't want to leave. Mr. Bordino was preaching to the wind. The dogs were moving in packs, and rats were the size of cats. I shot up the street lights. The weather was cooling down. After a week of marriage, I told my wife I wanted to go out for a while. Marriage was getting to be a drag. She said, "Okay, come back soon."

I hung out around the corner. The weather was cold at night. I played cards in the club where it was warm. The boys had some hot food, and life was good. I started getting a hard on. It was time to go home and see the bride.

The house was cold, and she was under ten blankets and a rug. She said, "The fucking heat stopped."

I went next door to see what the problem was. There was no oil in the tank. The next day the man delivered oil. The house was cozy, and it wasn't so bad. I had a lot of ammunition, and I would go into the basement to fire guns at targets. My wife would join in, and she got the hang of it.

Then the rats started coming into the house. I would go down to the cellar and light a candle in a spot that gave me a clear shot. I placed a hot potato near the candle and waited. The smell of the hot potato soon got their attention, and once they started eating, I would open fire. When I missed, they hid in the junk. The next day I cleaned up the junk and put it in the cellar next door. I had an open shot from any spot in the cellar. It was good practice, shooting at running rats. I improved my firing to the point where I could hit a rat running at top speed.

I had to let my wife move in with her parents. We were approved for an apartment in the projects in Canarsie. We moved in, but I held onto the old place. I got in touch with a man named Davie Gold who was running a floating craps game. This guy had been on death row for years, but he caught a break and beat the rap. Years before, when I shined shoes, I took notice of him. He was my size. He had black hair, black eyes, was slim, and wore the finest clothes. I knew he was a killer, and I wanted to be like him and be respected out of fear.

As I spoke to Davie Gold, I looked into his eyes and was hungry to read his thoughts. The blackness of his eyes went flat, and he shut me out. I said, "Davie, I have a spot for the games." He gave me a figure, I accepted, and then he asked if I wanted to run the food concessions. I said yes, while the craps game was at my house. I also told him that the house was coming down in a few months.

The craps game came to my house. When the game was over, I swept the garbage down the steps into the cellar, and the rats were delirious. I took off from the barbershop for a while because business was down due to the flight of the Jews and some Italians. I was taking in cash from the game and doing a couple of scores with Charlie. I was at the house during the day, and guys would come down for laughs. Most of the guys were clowns but were good looking and had girlfriends who slipped them a few bucks. Most of them lived at home. I loved to fuck with them, and I was always looking to set them up.

I moved up to the second floor of the apartment and took all the furniture. Every ten minutes somebody had to take a piss, and when he stepped into the bathroom, I would yell, "Freeze!" The ex-con would yell, "He's got a gun." I fired a shot through the door. This scene was to die for. I failed to consider that the tub was cast iron, and a couple of strays were dancing around his feet. He jumped into the piss bowl.

I waited till things got back to normal. I had an old TV on the table, and the intelligentsia would sit around watching *Rooty Kazootie*, a screwball show that six-year-old kids watched. I yelled, "I hate you, Rooty," and shot six rounds into the TV.

I spent a lot of time blasting away at rats. I had to sneak up on them. They were fattened up from all that food from the craps game. I had gathered about a dozen of them and hung them up by their tails at the window so the boys could get some target practice. Four of us lined up and opened fire. The rats exploded and got their revenge. I told the guys to get ready for a safari. One guy piped up, "What's a safari?" I said, "It's like a blow job."

To get to the cellar, we had to go outside and then inside the building next door and down to the basement. As we entered, the rats were scurrying around. I took a shot into the ceiling, and the guys were shitting their pants. The door that separated both buildings was open, and we walked through it. The six of us looked at that huge pile of garbage. I closed the door behind them and said, "Take out your guns, and open fire on that pile."

They were frozen as I emptied my gun into that pile of garbage. The rats stampeded, and there was pandemonium. The door was closed, and the guys fought to get it open. In the meantime, I reloaded and started shooting again. They tore the door down and went up the stairs, out the front door, and into their cars. I outdid myself on that one.

I became more diabolical and tried to perform in a manner that would elicit a response, as long as the person displayed emotion to the hilt. Imagine someone playing Russian roulette with your head. That would be kind of funny.

The guy who took the clowns down was a bank robber, and he was as dumb as they come. A friend told me once when they entered the bank, his mind went blank, and he had to take his hand and lead him around. He once made the front page of the newspapers, but I can't remember his name. I asked him to take a fresh bunch of assholes down. I spent a couple of days trapping rats. I still had a refrigerator, and I laid it down on the floor and shot some holes through the door. The rats were hopping around in the refrigerator.

As the intellectuals rolled in, asking about the refrigerator being on the floor, I said, "I shot a stool pigeon, and I want to feed him to the rats." I asked for help to stand the refrigerator up, and they looked at the bullet holes in the door. Then they looked at the ex-con, who told them I was nuts. I screamed, "Pick up the fucking refrigerator!" They swung into action. The refrigerator was standing, and I said, "Do you want to see what a stool pigeon looks like?" I was waving my gun, and suddenly I opened fire. The gunfire and the shock of the rats running as I opened the door put the fear of Jesus in their hearts. They were holding onto each other like a school of fish.

I must say that was the best of the best. The world can produce an army of comedians, and instead of putting them in jail, you can put them on a stage on Broadway. My wife was pregnant, and things were looking up. Then my mother died a couple of months before my daughter was born. We moved into the new projects in Canarsie a few miles from the barbershop. My daughter was born, and I never loved anything more than that kid. ·

Al and I got busted trying to yank a safe out of a supermarket. A few months later, we were sentenced to one year at Riker's Island. It was an eye opener. The correctional officers were not to be fucked with. Say one thing shitty to them, and they would hit you with a Billy club or a black jack. Walk into the mess hall talking, and they would sneak up on you and bust you on the side of the head. Al had a lot of strength from working all those years throwing cases of soda like tea bags. He was not a vicious guy. He was like a kid and had no meanness.

We hung out together and had common sense debates about things in general. He was a born interrogator. I loved to get deep into a subject that was bogus and defend it to the max. Debating the bastard was very frustrating. Since I was a barber, I was transferred to the hospital and given a box of tools. As soon as the inmates and guards found out that I was a barber and a good one, I was treated like royalty. Basically my job was going from floor to floor cutting heads.

The hospital was a dumping ground for skids. If any hospital had a bum who was near death, they would ship them to Riker's Island to die on the books. The death count meant nothing to the jail, and some inmates were very cruel. Some were bedridden with bed sores when it was time to change their bandages. Some were comatose as they ripped the bandages off. I looked at their faces, and I could see the pain in their eyes. Dead or alive, they knew they were in the hands of the devil. The inmates scooped out the pus with a wooden spoon, put on clean gauze, and bandaged the wound. They would look at me and say, "Now that's a nice job."

I spent a lot of time working with the drug addicts on the top floor. These addicts were not prisoners, and they were given a chance to detox. One hundred percent were Chinese, and they had money to buy cigarettes. I charged a pack for a regular haircut, two for a special. The difference was regular had no apron and no powder, and I gave a little more attention to the specials. I had a bench plus a chair. For the five who were on the bench, I finished the haircuts in five minutes. I took time with the specials. Chinese hair was hard to cut, and you had to be a master to cut their hair. After a couple of hundred, I was able to give a good haircut.

I didn't smoke, but my partner smoked a couple of packs a day. The rest I gave to the skids. I charged the screws a pack, and they knew that I was giving the skids the cigs. The inmates knew the skids had social security, and they took advantage in any way they could. Most were arrested for humane reasons. The winters were brutal, and their feet were black from frostbite. Others were beaten half to death. On court day in the hospital, the inmates came before the judge. They pleaded with the doctor, who then told the judge how much time the inmate needed to recuperate. The doctor said six months, and the judge nodded his head. It was common-sense justice. Today that would be a lawsuit.

I was given a sheet of names that were scheduled for a haircut at the morgue. A fat slob with a bloody plastic glove pointed to a stiff. The guy was covered in huge stitches. I asked if he was going into a hole or going home. He said he was destined for the funeral home. This was not the first time I was about to give a haircut to a guy without a brain. The barbershop was loaded with zombies. The fat slob sewed the eyebrows to the hairline. I did my best. I cut him a few times. Needless to say, but I'll say it anyway, he did not bleed. The rest of them got a fast job.

I looked forward to seeing my wife at the hospital visiting room. I had a phone, and we talked about what our future could be like. I painted a picture that made the angels smile. It took a couple of hours by bus, train, and ferry boat to get to Riker's. Once I wanted my mother to die so I would not feel guilty, and now I wanted my wife to die so I would not feel guilty. A pattern was forming. Could it be that someday I might wish for the death of my child? Nothing was strange anymore. I started to understand that the harder the treatment, a form of absolution ran through my blood.

The hospital was a great place with so much to do. They had a wing for inmates who needed protection. There was an internal investigation into the police department, and twenty or so captains, sergeants, and bagmen were indicted and convicted and sent to Riker's. I was soon cutting their hair. I was shocked to see the tall, blond, blue-eyed Irish cops. They looked like German prisoners of war. They had the faces of angels and a stare of a Monsignor.

Their crimes were understandable to me. The mob and gamblers were told to conduct themselves. They were charged like any other business. They kept the murder count down, and the streets were safe. I understood that taking orders was ingrained in these men. They acted like it was a German prisoner of war camp and they were still taking orders from the high command as a sign of respect. Their speech pattern was a lot different when they kicked my ass. They differentiated between a gambler and a common thief. I had pled guilty to being a common thief.

Riker's is where I met Henry Caron, my true partner in crime. He worked in a section of the hospital that dealt with food. Al had introduced Henry to me. He was around five years younger than me. Henry was French, and he had one blind eye. He was a natural gangster and was ready to put his life on the line. When I met him, he looked like a fucked-up kid. I gave him a haircut, and that improved his looks. I listened to his conversation while I gave him a haircut. He had the proper attitude to be a heist man. I told him to come to the barbershop when he got out.

I kept up the payments on the apartment and still had it. My wife came to the prison, and she was so hot looking that I almost passed out.

I put in my time, and my wife came to pick me up. We took the ferry and went to her mom's house. I walked in, and my daughter was stunned. She started to scream and never stopped crying. We took the kid home, and I was very happy. I took off a couple of weeks and hung out with the wife and kid. I still had the car, and we would go to the movies. I had to see the boys. Al was out. Charlie popped in, and we talked. I had to make some sense of this thing we had going if someone stole a truck. One must have a buyer for the goods. Most mob-connected men had a way to sell any type of merchandise. Made men were unapproachable, and rightfully so.

A man who was dealing on the side to pick up a few bucks, when he was confronted with a truck full of sides of beef, threw them for a loop. They wanted a box of steaks they could sell. If you take a chance with a local thief, word spreads like wildfire in thiefdom. That's a dangerous move. The sneaks keep their eyes and ears open for information. The floating craps game and the card rooms were where the dumb ones bragged about this or that in the open. It was not long before the detective picked you up and kicked you in the balls and shins to get you to come up with some information.

Dealing with racketeers was a risky business. The name of the game was payrolls and making connections with a made man. I told Henry I had a guy who had information, but I didn't tell him it was mob connected. I was told that if he heard that his name was on the street, I wouldn't last twenty-four hours. He gave me a number to call, and then I could never use that number again. I called and was told about a panel truck at a certain loading platform. Henry and I took the panel truck. The driver remained with one of us. He was cuffed with a blanket on his head. A half hour later, he was released. What was in the truck, I do not know.

A month later, he came to the barber shop and gave me fifteen grand for a haircut. I asked him for work. He said, "Don't get hungry." Then he said to me, "When I give you something, it will be a sure thing."

Henry was looking to do something with a young kid. The kid had a payroll score, and Henry came to the shop to pick up his gun that he had in his box. I never saw the kid he was working with. The guy with the payroll didn't show up, so they decided to rob the bank. The kid walked in, went to the teller, got a bag of money, and walked out the door. When they came back, Henry put the gun back in his box, introduced the kid to me, and then left. Since I had customers, we said nothing. Henry said he would see me the next day, and then he left with the kid.

The next day Charlie and Al came around, which was usual. I told them what had happened. The next day Henry passed by my apartment, and Al and Charlie showed up to see if they could get a few bucks. The kid and Henry passed out a couple of hundred each. My wife witnessed the exchange, but she did not get anything. After a while, they all left.

The kid was spending money, and someone tipped off the cops. They picked him up, took him to the police station, and put him in a lineup. The teller said it was not him. The other teller who witnessed the robbery also said it was not him. They released the kid. The kid was lucky.

Henry came around with another guy who was on parole and was wanted for violation. He hung out with Henry. It was one of those things. Henry liked the punk and told him a lot of shit. That gave us a lot of grief. Henry was spending money on the punk.

He asked me if my wife would dye his hair. I talked her into it, and that was a big mistake on my part. I dragged my wife into a gang of problems. I finally told Henry the guy had to go. He stole a car and took off. Two weeks later, two detectives picked me up at the shop and told me that they wanted to question me at the Seventy-Third Precinct. They asked me about the bank robbery. I told them I was working when that happened. Then they started with the good cop and the bad cop, and the good cop said, "Listen, I don't want you to get hurt. I am a Jew." I said, "Fuck you, Jew." He looked at me and then walked out the door.

My hands were cuffed, and I heard people running. They kicked the door open and then beat the fuck out of me with a rubber hose. They lifted my arms above my head and pounded on my ribs. Then they stopped and ran out the door. The good cop came back in and told me to use my head. "They won't stop beating you."

I was never more ready to take on the fucks. They came down with a rubber hose on my shoulders. They left again, and this time they took a half hour before they came back in. One of the cops yelled, "Beat the fuck to death."

I said nothing. I remembered when they had me hanging by my wrists. The more I cursed them out, the more it reinforced the idea that I was not about to bury myself, plus I wasn't looking too good. They would have to explain the shape I was in. The Jew detective came back in and told me he was taking me home. On the way back, the detective told me there was a rat who gave me up and said I was the mastermind of my fucked-up gang. I said, "What witness?"

He said, "John Beck."

I said, "No more."

I went home that day and then went to the barbershop. My dad looked at me and told me to go home. I left the shop and went to the house. My wife and I went over what John Beck knew. I brought out the fact that she dyed his hair at my request. She also was around when Henry passed out the money to the guys.

The cops had no case. They needed a gun. They picked up Charlie and Al. Charlie got roughed up, and he gave up the gun. The cops got security to open my door at daybreak. They moved in fast and put guns to my head. I was let out of the house and taken to the police station—the Seventy-Fifth Precinct. Charlie, Al, and I were handcuffed to the chair. I knew Charlie got rid of the gun, and I also knew that Charlie had never done any time before. I asked him, "Did you give up the gun?"

He pointed to his mouth and said, "I told the cops that the gun belonged to John Beck."

He had no idea that he buried six guys, and himself. Al pointed to me and said, "Look what they did to Mike." He realized what he did and could not look at anyone in the eye. A week later, we were taken to Raymond Street Jail in Brooklyn.

The agents came to interview me and told me if I didn't confess, they would charge my wife with bank robbery. I also remember saying, "Is you going to lock up my daughter?" I said, "No deal."

The story was building up each day in the media, and it went from page ten to page one. I went to court for a hearing, and as I was standing before the judge, someone handed me the *Daily News*, and there was a front-page picture of my wife with the headline, "Gun Moll." Upon seeing her photo, I went ape shit. The next day the headline was, "Mastermind Goes Berserk."

Whatever money I had, I gave to my wife to pay for a lawyer. Raymond Street Jail was no joke. The screws went around fucking with people. They were quick to jump into a cell and work you over. My wife came to visit me, and I told her the case against her was weak. I told her to tell the truth and that the truth would set her free. She had no knowledge of anything—just bullshit things that were said after the fact. My older sister came to visit me every other day and had to stand in the rain and snow.

Weeks turned into months. The case was weak, and the feds were looking for Hannigan, Henry's partner. Al, Charlie, Henry, and I made no confession, but they took Charlie to trial for bank robbery. He was given a twenty-year sentence. They offered him a deal to testify against me and the rest. The fact was, Al and Charlie had no knowledge of the crime until the day after the robbery when they accepted the money from Henry. I was advised that a payroll was to be taken, not a bank robbery. I aided and abetted when I allowed the guns to be stored in my shop.

After the conviction, Charlie regained his dignity and put the heat on me to tell my wife not to testify about the bank robbery, in which we all were indicted. I told him I would not do anything to jeopardize her. I said we were all getting buried for nothing, and I was not going to bury her.

I was severed from the case because my wife was to testify. She did nothing, she got no money, and she never admitted to seeing the guns. She said I told her not to open the box. She admitted that she saw a few hundred spread around. That alone said that we had nothing to do with the crime when the take was in the thousands. We had no share in that money, and as far as being a mastermind, in actuality I was a masturbator. If someone cracked my head open, thousands of little pussies would spill out. If I had my prick in my hand and a naked lady was in front of me, I would find that snatch lickity split. That was the extent of my intelligence.

I had solace knowing that the FBI never intended to put my wife in jail. As for me, the FBI knew I was cutting hair at the time of the robbery. They were remiss in their duty in portraying me as a mastermind. That portrayal earned me an additional fifteen years to my sentence. I could have beaten the rap with a half-assed lawyer, but I was tapped out. I may have got some time, but after thinking it over, I was guilty. I was always guilty. A dog will always do what a dog does. The thing was, Henry was a man. He was brave, and that combination of character, I had to respect.

My wife was safe, and she came twice a week to visit me. I would bust a nut just looking at her. The hell I put her through surpassed anything that was in store for me. I was placed in a two-man cell at that time. The jail cells were two blacks or two whites. I spent two years sitting in a cell twenty-three hours a day. Breakfast was served in a mess hall that had ten tables to serve hundreds of men. Eating time was five minutes after you sat down. The last meal was in your cell, and lights out was at ten. Sunday was church time. I went to every church—Protestant, Catholic, and a few others. The Catholic Church was fun. The altar boy was a little fuck, and he hated the cons. He would be dressed up in his uniform, glancing at me, and I would give him the evil eye. I had a pocket full of spitballs, and when the priest had his back to me, I would try to hit him in the head with spitballs. He was livid with rage.

The confession was on Saturday. I loved to confess my sins. I would tell him a fuck story with a black girl that sent him through the roof. He said that I was evil, like a rotten branch on a tree to be cut down and burned to ashes. But he kept coming back, and I had to change the story. I told him that my girl was still black, maybe a little blacker. She showed me her big black pussy through the window.

The best thing was when the coffee man came by each morning. I got the *Daily News* and a May west, and I would sit in front of the cell door and read the paper and drink coffee. In one of my speeches, I was bragging that I could bust out of this joint. Word got back to the warden, and I was arrested and placed on death row. I said to myself, "If I keep this shit up, I'll never get to see my daughter until she is eighty years old."

I was under twenty-four-hour surveillance. The coffee man said, "You made headlines." He gave me the paper and showed me the front page. A screw was on the jailhouse roof with a machine gun. I was called to the hearing by the three deputies. I walked into the room, and there were three deputies in uniform. I looked at them and said, "Who the fuck am I, Humphrey Bogart?" They busted out laughing.

The charges were read by a sergeant. Count one was conspiring to engage others to escape, count two was gathering saw blades, and count three was planning to destroy government property. They asked, "How do you plead?"

I said, "Not guilty." As for count one, why would I want to engage with some fucked-up inmate when I had a wife? Count two, would you smuggle saw blades up your ass? The captain said, "Not guilty. You will remain on death row." I liked death row. I had a single cell and was able to walk on the flats. I ate my meals in my cell, and to find things to do, I decided to feed the cons on the tier. I had one blanket, one rock-hard pillow painted with fire retardant, a sheet, and a two-inch mattress. I tore the sheet into two narrow strips.

I told the guy who handed out shit paper that I needed extra shit paper. At first he said no, but when he found out that I was a gang leader and was on death row under surveillance, he thought twice about refusing me. Plus I told him these guys would pull his arms off if I told them to. He gave me as much as I wanted. I told him I had to wrap up twenty sandwiches at night, and I could see the wheels turning in his head. I yelled, "The shit paper man doesn't want to give me paper." He said okay.

I saved food from breakfast, and I got extra loaves of bread and a bag of prunes. For lunch I stacked up more food. They gave me what I wanted, and when the lights went out, I made the sandwiches. I made about twenty sandwiches, tied them to the sheet strip, and sent them down. It was quite a feat. I kept the minds of killers who see the passage of time getting closer to the day that turns their brains into soup. I had a work force of killers feeding killers-to-be BBQ themselves. When we were on the flats, I spoke to all of them. I wanted to know what they did and how they did it. It was like being there. Some were very descriptive.

Years later when I was in Atlanta, I read in the *Daily News* a short story about someone who was electrocuted. This guy's story was about a senseless killing. He was a big man who had the smallest prick I ever saw. I also recollected the warning the judge gave me, that one day I might end up in the electric chair. That was a sobering thought. I feel no need to kill and have no anger. This is my first book, and I hope it's not the last.

I was locked up for quite a while when word got to me that John Beck was in lock up. I had a shot at him. Al, Charlie, and I waited to get to the church on the weekend. After church we were able to walk past his cell and put the heat on him. He was terrorized. I told him that I would fill his head with lead. He said he was sorry. I told him to tell the truth.

In his cell, John Beck wrote a statement refuting his testimony. The lawyer went before the court, and the judge said that the witness was in fear for his life and threw the statement out. I never told a fucking thing to anyone. I was transferred to the Bronx County jail to be set up by another informant. The government knew that John Beck fucked up the case, and now they needed a new witness to say this or that.

It made it harder for my wife to visit me. She came a few times a week. My older sister also came to see me, and I told her I was trying to get the deputy to give me an affidavit that I was not talking about my case to anyone.

The deputy said, "I have no way of knowing if you're talking or not."

I said, "If I'm going through all this trouble, why would I talk about my case?"

The place was full of material witnesses. At night the place was crawling with rats, the four-legged kind. I had food and heavy books. I placed the books on the floor, and I set the book so that when I pulled a string, the book rained down on the rat. I was tossing rats everywhere. No one was safe. A couple of months later, I was back in Raymond Street Jail, and my codefendants were transferred to the Federal House of Detention. I remained in the Raymond Street Jail till the trial. Hannigan was arrested, and the feds got a confession from him. He also said that he did not know me and that we never planned anything. He said that Henry went to the barber shop to get the gun.

Now the feds had a confession that implicated me. When Hannigan found out that no one confessed, he recanted what he confessed to. In the long term, I used that confession to make my case, but I did ten years. The judge ruled that the confession was legal, except that the names of the defendants were not to be used. Instead, my name was changed to an X. Hannigan took the fifth, and I got fucked. I had no way to challenge the confession. I was denied my constitutional right to confront the witness and was taken to trial. A blue-ribbon jury was selected, and I'm sure they could spot a bank robber when they saw one, because they all look alike.

I was convicted and received twenty years in the federal penitentiary in Atlanta, Georgia.

My wife's case was dismissed, and she came to visit me at the Federal House of Detention. She said she wanted to wait for me. I told her I was facing ten years for sure and she must divorce me. They never give parole to bank robbers. The worst part was that I couldn't tell her that I would change my ways. I said, "Think about it. Don't throw your life away."

It took a few days to get to Atlanta. We made stops and stayed overnight in prisons. It was not like the time when I made my trip to Paris Island. Al was in Atlanta, and I thought about him with his wife, and two kids, and he was innocent. As for myself, I believed that as long as I remained a criminal, I must take the good with the bad, and I made up my mind to have a good attitude. The weather was nice, the yard was excellent, and the food was to die for. There were two baseball fields and a wall twenty feet high that made wonderful handball courts. I got in the best of shape that I ever was. I played like a child. I would go to sleep and play a perfect game in my dreams. The street was a struggle, and here everything was free. To compound all of this, they paid us to work, and we made a lot of money.

In Atlanta in the fifties, if you worked hard, you were able to make over fifty dollars a month, when ice cream was twenty-five cents a pint.

The screws we called boss were okay. This one boss man stood in the middle of a great big hallway that divided the cell blocks. Each block held hundreds of men. When the mess hall was over, the men were allowed to go to the yard or to their cells. The boss man stood like a wooden Indian with his arms across his chest, looking at every con as they passed. When he pointed at someone, a second boss pulled him to the side and shook him down for food, and sure as shit, he was busted. I got no mail. It was a long month. Al and I were separated. I started making friends, and when the month was over, I was assigned to a cell block.

The prison held twenty-four hundred men. The cell block had four tiers with four-story-high windows. Each cell had five double bunks, with one toilet, one sink, plus a small sink to brush your teeth, a headphone for a radio, one blanket, two sets of clothes, and an army jacket. I hit a cell that was mostly southerners. The time I spent in the marines gave me insight, and I knew what they thought about Yankees. With a little bullshit, I fit right in. I started talking shit, and they loved it. Most had a little time. They asked right away how much time I had. I said, "Twenty years."

One big old boy said, "What did you do, rob a bank?"

I said yes, and the last thing I would say was that I was innocent. I made myself a bad motherfucker. I asked, "What about you?"

A moonshiner busted out, "He's a chicken fucker, watch your ass."

I said, "He could try. I have a razor blade up my ass."

I was lucky. Most moonshiners were older men, and the place was mostly white-collar crimes, tax evasion, spies, soldiers, bank robbers, and narcotics. There were no rapist, unless it was on government reservation.

There were two brothers who were convicted for rape that had taken place on government land. I used to see them talking from a barred window. One was a real young kid. The young brothers raped a girl and let her go. Ike was the president. He gave the order to execute, and they were fried in a state prison. It was count time. Once the count was clear, we walked to the mess hall. They had ten stations, and I was looking for a short line. I spotted one and made a beeline for it. Within seconds, a hand was around my neck, and I left the floor. The boss was a monster. He put me down and said, "Do you want to start a riot? This is not New York City; this is the state of Georgia, and you have broken the law."

The state was segregated, and I knew it. I looked around. I was in a sea of black people, and every black was laughing at me. Not one white said a thing. I just learned that if you don't watch your ass, someone will steal it. The boss continued talking, and the blacks kept laughing. I said out loud, "Lock me up or let me go." That was the best move to shut him up. He took a long look at me and pointed to the white section. Word got out about what I said.

I was dejected that no one sent me a letter. The prison had a large population of Italians. Most were in the drug trade. I had no opinion on who does what. I just knew after two years in the county jail that dope breeds rats. Every sale made is a paper trail. The feds fatten up a dealer to the point where they do sixty years or walk out and work off their time. Either way it's a losing proposition.

Al lived in a different block. Henry and Hannigan went to Lewisburg, and Charlie went to Kansas.

Atlanta had good food, and you could get fat if you sat on your ass and did nothing. After chow I went out into the yard to see Al. When Al was in the Federal House of Detention, he got to know a lot of main characters in the mob. Like I said, he was a likable guy and always looking to get ahead. With his height, he made a good impression. The Irish were respected. Most were tough, took no shit, and loved to kill. The war in Boston was deadly. I was very cautious of who I hooked up with. I looked for guys who were into sports. Handball and weightlifting were the main sports for me. With less talk and a lot of work, I kept away from jailhouse politics. I was twenty-nine, and to me it was a vacation.

My wife sent me a letter with divorce papers and said she was taking my advice. I remember going to the office and talking to the counselor about signing the divorce papers. He said, "You don't have to sign the papers." I looked at him, took the pen from his hand, and signed the divorce papers. Immediately I felt like a boulder dropped off my back. My feelings for my wife ended, and the feeling was profound. I only wanted freedom from any responsibility. Finding, fucking, and forgetting lust was what I wanted.

Al got involved with the church, and he talked about miracles. He was really fucked up in the head. He wrote letters to his wife and two kids, and had me listen to every word. The effort that went into those letters was mind boggling. If you read that letter to a tombstone, no matter what was buried there, they would come to life. Like God said, it takes a crippled mind to raise the dead. I hooked up with a body-building and weight-lifting team, and we protected our spot in the yard. The yard remained open in the summertime till 7:00 p.m. at night.

Al gave me a spoon of coffee each night. I had no money, and I had to wait six months and have a clean record before I was permitted to work in the cotton mill. I told my family that I had a paying job and had no need for money. My wife sent me no mail and no photos of my daughter. I decided to let my family know that I did not want any information about my wife or child.

Six months went by, and I started working in the factory. I worked my way up to running a spinning machine. The noise was loud, and the boss man was tough. He hated Yankees, but I played by the rules for a while. I needed that job because it made the time go by faster; I could buy cookies and coffee. The food was good, and there was no need to buy anything else. I had what I needed. I would buy a carton of cigarettes for Al because he had a low-paying job. He was more interested in playing baseball and was on the main team.

When spring training came around, the Major League teams would come to the institution to play the jailhouse team. Al had a uniform, hat, and shoes. The problem was, the shoes were too small. The spikes glistened in the sun. The guy kept me laughing. I liked Al from the time I met him. He squeezed his feet into the shoes and prayed for the pain to go away. I suggested that he cut a slice over each toe so that the toes could free themselves. He said that the shoes were government shoes. I said, "Wrap some tape around the shoes, and that will cover the toes that stick out. The fat slob who runs the athletic department never watches the games and can't prove that you cut your shoes."

Pain defied the rules. He sliced and diced, and you could see the birth of little toes. They were prying their way out. A shock wave hit me. His feet looked like two huge crabs. He was hopping around, the crabs were alive. I said, "Wrap them fucking feet up."

He managed to last a week with his freedom feet. He hit the ball out of the park and was breaking the factory windows. Two weeks before the big game, someone tipped the boss man off that Al cut his shoes. The boss went dog shit and told Al he was off the team. The guys wanted to beat the symbols of our imprisonment. Some started rumors that the shit would hit the fan.

Everybody liked Al. You couldn't help but like him when he looked you in the eyes and you saw the inquisitive stare of a child who got a solid hit. When he wrote letters home, they were written in an expressive manner. He would underline the sentences in different colors, red being the most intense. He had to teach the sensor how to read each and every letter.

The athletic boss hated all the pressure put on him. I told to knock it off. "The crackers will back up their own and make your life a living hell." I said, "Fuck that game, and tell the boss that you will pay for the shoes." The major league team came in and kicked the shit out of the con team.

Al was one of the best handball players. He was great to watch. His range and agility were an art form. The mob bosses were being convicted and sentenced to big numbers. Vito Genovese was sentenced to twenty years and entered Atlanta. Frank Costello was sentenced for interstate gambling was sent to Atlanta. Joe Valachi was convicted on drug charges and was sent to Atlanta. Mickey Cohen, a racketeer, was convicted of tax evasion and sent to Atlanta. The colonel, a Russian spy, was sent to Atlanta. Sobel, a spy, was convicted, received thirty years, and sent to Atlanta. Sobel was connected to Ethel and Julius Rosenberg.

The principals were arriving at intervals to add spice to the intrigue. The rumors were being played out in the media, and the Federal Institution of Atlanta was being scrutinized by the eyes and ears of the world. Al kept me abreast of the latest inside stories. In the meantime, I went back to work at the factory, and each morning I was greeted by a black man called Mr. Right. As soon as I passed through the doors he would say, "Right," and I would say, "Right, right," and he would say, "Right, right, right." This went on all day long. Everybody fucked with Mr. Right. There were dozens of guys who joined in on the bullshit, and the poor bastard must have said that word a thousand times a day.

Boss Mathis wanted to catch me smoking, and I let him think I was a smoker. Once I had my machine working, I would spot him hiding behind a cart that was loaded with bobbins. I would go to the shit house and looked out the door to see if he was around. I cut back in and held my hand like I had a smoke. Boss Mathis cut in, stuck his nose into the urinal, smelled my hands, and stared at me. He had crystal blue eyes and said, "I'll get you." He would walk around looking for cans and wires.

I knew an inmate who made stingers. He hooked me up with a stinger to heat the water so I could have coffee. The element was the coil that had to be submerged in the water. If not, the element would burn and cause a fire, and that was very dangerous. The factory with its cotton particles was like a bomb, and any spark could cause an ignition that would have killed over one hundred men. No one actually explained the danger to me. I was dying for a cup of coffee, and as I was boiling the hot water, the stinger rose from the water and started to glow like a light bulb. I shoved the coil with my foot back down into the water and pulled the plug from the socket. I took the stinger and broke it up. The danger was so close that it shook the shit out of me. I was wrong to ever use one. I put the inmates and the prison personnel in jeopardy.

Back in the yard, Al told me that Joe Valachi was an informant for the FBI. A couple of connected men from Buffalo told Vito Genovese Valachi was an informant. My next-door neighbor was asked by someone close to Vito Genovese to pull his jacket. Johnny was a good guy who I liked a lot. Friends of Valachi who were stand-up guys were shaking in their shoes.

A couple of months before, Joe Valachi and his sidekick were using my bench to work out. My crew was getting ready for a workout, and I told Joe that he had to get his own spot. He reacted in anger, threw the weight down, and gave me a look of hate. I had disrespected him, and I was responsible for what happened to me. The good thing was, no one was around, and his sidekick had to keep his mouth shut. If anyone had heard me refuse him, I would have been in deep shit. I explained to his friend that Joe was a good man and let it go at that. Things improved between us. Valachi knew he didn't need any more enemies. John pulled his jacket, and Vito read the jacket. The FBI had to tell the warden that the prisoner was an informant. The reason was to keep people separated who are a threat to each other. Word got around that Vito gave Joe the kiss of death.

At that time, I had started my vacation, which meant that I could stay in my cell or go out in the yard. My door remained open, and I just enjoyed lying around. I needed to relax. Johnny asked me to go for a walk with him. I said, "Johnny, I need to relax."

That decision saved my life. He would have loved to have taken me out along with Johnny. As Johnny was walking along with a few guys, Joe Valachi broke off a piece of pipe from a building that was under construction, and as Johnny was walking by, Valachi struck him from behind, blow after blow. Johnny hung on for a few days and then passed away.

Joe Valachi calmly walked up to the boss, and said, "I just killed a man." Joe was taken from the prison, put in protected custody, and eventually went before a congressional committee. Joe Valachi knew John pulled his jacket, and Joe got his revenge. Now he had the opportunity to dismantle the organization before the people of the United States. Vito was a gentleman. He sat around the handball court sunning himself. I got to talk to him about Al and the crazy crap that we did together. He liked the fact that we went to trial and made no deal and that we were bank robbers.

Most made men followed the rules and made no deals. It would have been easy to point a finger at someone else and let him do the time. To do that is to erode the soul. You pay either way. I never asked for favors, and I kept the bullshit rolling. When I challenged Al to a game, I called him all kinds of names and said I'd kick his ass. A lot of funny stuff came out of my mouth.

Mickey Cohen arrived from California. In his younger days, he was a professional fighter. He was five-foot-six in height and slim. He loved the limelight, and his exploits filled the newspapers, like the gang wars and the attempt assassinations. His house was bombed. One of his associates, Johnny Stompanato, was involved with Lana Turner.

Lana Turner gave the gossip columns plenty to write about. That stormy relationship put Mickey into the headlines. Subsequently, the daughter of Lana Turner stabbed Johnny to death. Mickey eventually was charged with tax evasion, convicted, and sentenced to fifteen years in Atlanta. He was placed in a cell next door to me, and I liked him immediately. He was a down-to-earth guy who tried to get along. His problem was that he was too nice. Most see that as a weakness, and they stormed his cell. The line outside of his cell was long. They had one thing in common; they wanted money. He took their names. This went on every day. He had his cell scrubbed with steel wool, and without a doubt he had a phobia for germs. Each night the boss let four men out to take a shower. The first time I showered with him, I was amazed by the amount of soap he used. He covered his body like a snowman. He would use a complete bar of soap. Each day after lockup, he would read newspapers from around the country, and every ten minutes he would wash his hands. You could hear the sound of toilet paper as it spun around in the holder.

He had a job handing out tools, and he managed a little shed next to a school for radio and television. I took a course and was accustomed to seeing Mickey come in, sit down, and watch TV. I was making stingers on the side.

There was a group of strong-arm guys, and they knew who to hit: the weak and those who had no friends. The inmate went to the commissary and took the groceries to his cell. He was greeted by a few unfriendly faces who roughed him up, and that was that. Someone told Mickey what happened. As smart as Mickey was, he was jail house stupid and didn't understand the rules, like do not talk about anyone. He also was infamous. The fact that he said the guy was a scumbag sealed his fate.

Word got out to the killer, who at that time was locked up for the theft. He was enraged when he found out what Mickey said. He managed to escape from lockup and made his way to the tool shed. Since Mickey was not there, he knew that he was watching TV. He broke off a piece of conduit pipe that was lying on the ground and walked into the classroom. At that time, Mickey was seated next to the post in a chair that had a high back. Nevertheless, he managed to strike several blows to the head.

I turned to see what was causing that noise. I thought Mickey was being hit by a newspaper. The assailant dropped the pipe and walked out. I ran to see what I could do. Mickey's head was covered with blood. I looked into his eyes. He was looking at me, and then his eyes dilated. The boss was speechless. He was in his sixties. He was a nice man but not the kind of man to protect you in a situation like this. Mickey was taken to the hospital, and after a long battle, he recuperated. He was partially paralyzed. He did his time, made it out, and I read somewhere that he died. I'm sure that those blows hastened his death.

Frank Costello entered Atlanta, joined the population, and lived up to his reputation as the prime minister of organized crime. He was a thinker, not a killer. As a celebrity, he had class. He built the mystique that the mob kept the neighborhood safe, and that was true. When close associates had problems, they were taken care of. I know for a fact that they killed their own. That was true but not for nothing. They were tried and found guilty. The Mob didn't kill good man. The safety of the organization was the fear of the kiss of death.

Sobel was related to Ethel and Julius Rosenberg, who were convicted spies in the forties. Sobel was given thirty years for whatever part he played in the espionage. I got to know Sobel, and I could see that he suffered greatly for what happened to him and his family. We spoke about things while we did our job. For the most part, he kept to himself. He wondered why I put myself in harm's way for a stupid bank job. It didn't make sense to him. And the fact that I seemed to be enjoying myself mystified him. He was a family man, and his wife waited thirty years for him. I'm sure he remembers me. He saw me do ten years and then return with ten years more. I read a story that he was released and returned to

California. I saw a picture of him and his wife, and that was the only time that I saw him smile.

There was another spy there, a Russian. The inmates showed him respect because he was a colonel in the Russian army. We felt he was doing his duty. His main game was bocce ball. At times I played with him, and the terminology I used for this shot or that shot made him laugh. The spot where I lifted weights was within earshot. I'm not sure when the colonel arrived, but there was an American pilot named Gary Powers who flew over Russia, taking photos of their military bases. He was shot down by Russian missile fire and then injured while being captured. The United States had been denying that we were spying, and after negotiations, Gary Powers was exchanged for the colonel. During the night the colonel was taken from Atlanta, and a short time later, both men were repatriated.

Al was transferred to Lewisburg Penitentiary, and I remained in Atlanta.

I had a cell mate who came out of DC, and his name was John. He was a serial killer. John was a master innovator. He was able to take machinery and improve its efficiency. This took place when I first arrived at Atlanta, and I was in a ten-man cell. The cell had a clock that had no visible sign of energy to propel it. John showed me the inner workings of the clock. He had patience. His Nordic mind knew that my sub intellect would never figure it out. The fuck was right. He would say in his insane voice, "You give up?"

I said, "I think I've got it." I told him I needed a little more time, but I was convinced that I would not figure it out. I put my mind to work.

I told the boss of the cell block that I was a professional barber. I told him, "I'll give you a haircut for a year if you show me how the clock works." He had the tools, and I gave him a haircut. He loved it. By law, an inmate can't display anything without the approval of the boss on duty. He gave me a copy of the mechanism. The clock ran from the pressure of a fan that sucked the air out of the cell, and it was out of sight. The amount of air was negligible.

I waited until John was irritated about something, and then I chirped out, "I know how you did it." He looked at me with confused laughter. I said, with the attention of the inmates, "Obscure air pressure."

One inmate said, "What the fuck is that?"

John wanted to put me on the kill list, but little by little, he was getting to like me and confide in me. He told me what he did over twenty years before. That put it into the forties. He would randomly kill blacks. He said that crime dropped off to an all-time low. No one left their homes. John was enrolled in a music class, and he made sure he made a black blow his trumpet. He wrote to the NAACP, explaining that he was doing God's work, and wanted their forgiveness. They responded that they had forgiven him.

I figured I would run a few tests on him. He lifted weights by himself. No one wanted him on their team. I would get him fucked up by using the word mother fucker. He would go into a tirade of profanity that showed a deep hatred that was profoundly insane. But that night, with trumpet in hand, he let the black man blow his horn. If I ever sell this book, I hope he's dead.

Before I arrived at Atlanta, there was an inmate who was a spy, and his name was Remington. He was involved with Alger Hiss, who was spying for the Russians. He was convicted and given five years for espionage. This supposed spy, in the custody of the US Attorney General, went to the canteen to buy a bag of groceries. At that time, a gang of thieves followed him to his cell. One kept a lookout while another crushed his skull with a brick and took his bag of food. They gorged themselves.

I received a letter from one of the perpetrators saying he would pray for me. He expressed love for my soul. I asked one of my cellmates, "Who the fuck is this guy?" He told me he was the one who killed Remington. I told my cellmate that I was thinking he might be in love with my asshole.

I hung with the Irish guys. The Boston crew was having a war in Boston against themselves. There was one hit after another. One got out and was dead a week or two later. They fell into a trap. They did a five- or ten-year sentence, walked out, and found out they didn't know what the fuck was going on. Guys were shot dead. Their old girlfriends were tied up with the enemy. Handsome and tough, they were waiting to take on the opposing crew. But treachery among the Irish was legendary.

Whitey Bulger came from Alcatraz when they closed the rock. Most were sent to Atlanta, and the rest were spread out among the institutions.

Whitey Bulger was a handsome, tough, and silent individual who seemed to have no friends. He worked out by himself. I would speak to him about whatever. He was blunt and to the point. I knew by his reputation that he was a bank robber. It seemed to me that bank robbery was beneath him. His demeanor was strong, and his stare was interrogatory. He was a work in progress. I managed to see his point of view. I knew from the beginning that the outcome was a sure thing.

There was an Irish inmate from Boston who told me someone wanted to die, but he could not bring himself to hang himself. He needed help to kill himself. The hangman told the hangee he had to pay up front. The hangee only had ten cartons of cigarettes, but the hangman wanted twenty-five. The hangman took the ten and was waiting for the rest. The weeks went by, and the hangee was getting cold feet. The hit was to be in the hangee's cell, but to do this, the hangman needed the cooperation of the hangee to complete a clean job. The hangee said, "Keep the cigarettes." The hangman did not want to hear that. "A deal is a deal." The hangee turned himself into the mental ward, and they shipped the fruitcake to Springfield.

The hangman got shitty with me because I irritated him. Each morning as I passed his cell, I said good morning in an upbeat voice. I decided not to talk to him. Years went by, and the day before his release, I went to him and wished him good luck. Two weeks later he was dead. I knew he was dead meat. His dispossession was the worst enemy he ever had.

Another young man from Boston was on my weightlifting team, and we were real tight. He was in good shape. I wanted to body punch with him. He told me if he beat me, he would hate me for letting him beat me. "I fight to kill, and once I start throwing punches, I can't stop until the guy is dead."

I said, "Forget about it, you're my buddy."

He had a girlfriend who was black, and he told me, "I'm telling you this because I love her. I want you to know that you are my friend, and I never want to hear you say anything about black woman." He left after the hangman and was killed himself.

Most of the killings were suicide. To know what you're up against and forge ahead into the halls of hell shows a complete denial of what's real.

Fear had a hand in the destruction of these warriors. Fear was the hardest thing to overcome. When someone makes a mistake and says to someone else behind his back that a person is a rat, hoping that someone else will do his dirty work, he is in grave danger. Another type is someone who has killed another inmate. He spends ten years in segregation and then comes out wild eyed, looking to see if someone is looking at him. He was haunted by the horror he had committed on someone else—the sight of bones sticking out of his neck. The thought that someone was about to do it to him was motivation to kill again, so that he could get peace in isolation. He struck again and walked away like nothing happened. I walked to the outside toilet. I experienced the excitement of seeing someone sitting on a toilet seat without a shirt and without a head. The flies beat me to him. If you relish that sight, you may be suited for a life of crime and grime.

At the rate of crime, it won't be long before we all will be voting for a warden. Signs are everywhere. The legislators disregard the true path to peace and prosperity. Good people who worked all their lives are hoping that their children will follow a path to success and happiness. Righteous people must band with righteous people to forge a path that is clear so people can follow. Discriminate against those who follow a life of division, and build a great love for one another. That will make you strong. Find a way to weed out the imposters who will join you.

Put up a fight. If you don't, it won't be long before they will be knocking at your door and telling you to get out of your own home. You can call 911 all day long, and the only ones who will come are those who bring nightmares. I have seen the good, I have seen the bad, and I have dined with evil. No matter what the mixture, it will always come out poison.

Atlanta was reasonable in the fifties, but nowadays the system has developed to a point that the inmates are being bred to overthrow the government. My hope is that I'm wrong. Since I never was right, there is a good chance I'm wrong now.

I did ten years and then left Atlanta in 1964. I took a flight to New York City and was scheduled to see the parole officer in ten days. I still had ten years left on my sentence. I got a job in a junkyard. Gabby was a childhood friend who gave me the job. He set me up in an apartment a mile from the junkyard. It was a place for his friends to get laid. The work was hard, but I did not mind working as long as it wasn't dull. The action was fast and furious. Gabby's good looks and style, light blue eyes, cowboy's outfit, and high-heeled boots put him in the six-foot range. I never saw him with a dog.

At first I wondered why he did not use the apartment. He told me that he promised them the time of their lives, but he was unable to produce. And me with the desire of a wildebeest. I hit on one of the broads, and she looked at me like I was a part on a greasy motor lying around on the ground.

There was a prostitute who came around looking to make a few bucks. Gabby gave the prostitute money to give me a blow job. He opened her mouth to show her teeth, and they were so perfect that I thought that they were false teeth. He was showing her teeth like it was a horse auction. She went down on me, and for a moment I thought I got my prick caught in a rat trap. Violence was perpetrated on me by a double-toothed girl as she tore the skin off the head of my cock. I had no way of popping. She continued with all the brutality she could muster up. The pain was excruciating, and she jumped on my cock like it was polish sausage. It was painful but not painful enough to stop the stars from exploding in my head.

At night when it was time to close, the junkers parked outside with families of blacks living in the cars. The nights were bitter cold, and they were standing around an oil drum burning tires to keep warm. The police understood and paid no attention. The kids were waiting for Gabby to come out and give them candy. Each and every morning he was there to give them money. They lined up, and he passed out five-dollar bills to each and every family. Gabby had an abused car lot. If a car looked respectable, he would put it on the side for sale.

Gabby had the best deal—no insurance and a mountain of plates. If the car broke down, there was a fifteen-dollar discount on the next seventy-five-dollar car, and if the car was stopped within the precinct, the cops came by the yard to pick up a small fee.

The boosters came around each day to sell merchandise that was snatched from some store. Al showed up with the Horn and took me to a prostitute's apartment. She was a head taller than I was. She took my cock out, and I popped three times. She asked if I had just got out of jail, and

I said, "Yes, and it will take me three or four shots before I settle down." I had four shots at her.

I asked Al if going straight was all bullshit. He told me that he tried. I asked, "What about God? Was that all bullshit?" I understood the need for God and that it kept people from going crazy. I was proud that I went through all that crap with nothing but my own fortitude. I trusted no one but myself.

Al hooked up with a money-making outfit. I was happy working. Kennedy airport was growing, and imports of all kinds, from gold to wigs, were lying around. A band of thieves blindly broke into the igloos hoping to hit the jackpot. Slowly and methodically, the groups organized. Bars became a location for information. Brooklyn was a place where someone knew someone who knew something. The tips became the person with the invoice. The trucks could not hide anymore. Passionate people's love of money and song, especially without paying for it, dominated while everyone was having fun driving stolen cars that were duplicated.

There was no sense having your lady shoplift and ruin a perfectly good handbag with a blood line. She could have it delivered via the guy who was still busting into igloos. I had a Puerto Rican girl living in my building, and she was hot. Her father was in jail. She spent her time fixing up her hair to impress me. When I got back from the junkyard, I was hotter than a junkyard dog. Her hair was kinky, and she was able to twist it around. At times it looked like a little garden. She kept me fucking, and I loved every bit of it. I never asked what she did all day, but I'm sure that she kept the tenants from moving out. I never gave her money; I gave her food. I hated paying for pussy. I wanted to feel that I loved her. Instead I gave her steaks at fire sale prices.

Gabby wanted me to cut cars. Once the car was turned over, I would cut the engine out. It was hot and dirty work. Gabby's friend Tom had a girlfriend who had a husband, and once a week, he took her to my place to get laid. She watched me cut the cars, and sparks were flying. The car caught fire. I was a pure animal. Tom was clinically clean, and at times she would step out of the car and do those things that drive men crazy. I would stand there and hold the torch, burning at an angle that appeared like I was holding my cock.

They left, and a while later, I got a call from Tom. He told me that his girl wanted to get laid by me, "so come quickly." I dropped the torch and took off. I was there in twenty minutes, standing in front of her. My face and hands were black with grease. I said, "I'll jump into the shower." She said, "No, fuck me now." She was pure white and Greek, and she had me on the ropes. I was so aroused that I penetrated her and came. I entered her again and fucked her hard. She was spasmodic. She had fingerprints all over her body. For six months, she wanted all the cock I could give her. I had the need for sex.

Things were rolling along at a slow pace. To make a few bucks on the side, I hooked up with a bootlegger who did time with me in Atlanta. He supplied me with a case of alcohol, and I broke it down to pints. I sold just enough so it wouldn't burn my ass. The junkyard was just the place. I knew enough blacks to get rid of a case a week. The guy who sold it to me had a business selling cheese, olive oil, and pure alcohol. The customer made their own type of drinks, and he would pass the yard, drop off a case, and put it in the trunk. I told no one. The blacks worked out of their homes.

I never increased the amount. I had enough money. They had other locations to buy alcohol. I didn't want to spend another ten years in jail for peanuts. I also knew I would never last ten years on parole. My only hope was to get off good. In the meantime, fucking was an addiction. Between the Greek and the Puerto Rican, it made me happy. I had enough money to buy little things for her, especially cosmetic jewelry. Gabby had nice stuff, and I paid little to nothing. The stuff was stolen, and some pieces were expensive. The junkies took eight cents on the dollar. My honey walked around the apartment with nothing on but the jewels. She was happy to sit around with me. I never pushed her around. I would tell her stories about the little children running away and the mother crying and happy endings. At times I told her one that she liked and wanted to hear it again. The problem was telling her a story, and when it was over, I had no idea what I said. I would ask her for details about the story so I would be able to piece it together. She thought the stories were true.

It's wonderful to have a lover who was a genius in bed and dumb like a bell when her feet hit the floor. Each day I would bring her things from Gabby's stash. I gave her expensive binoculars, and she went nuts when I took her to the roof of the apartment building that we were living in. It was ten stories high, and there was another building that also was ten stories high about a mile away. I showed her how to zoom in on people who were walking around naked. Some were in the shower. We both had binoculars, and we would sit on the edge of the roof spying. If I found someone doing something like getting laid, she wanted to go down to the apartment and fuck. She was obsessed, like she had to see the next chapter. I honestly believe that we could have been very happy together.

Henry was out, and it was closing in on 1965. I took up with a guy who was buying cars that were totaled. He would switch the VIN number to a car that was identical, a '63 or '64 Cadillac. They were going for five grand. A little here, a little there kept me floating. I would sit in some joints run by a legitimate man. Every guy I spoke to would say, "This is Tony's place." Once legit people heard that, they stayed clear of the place.

The Crystal Room was my favorite spot. It was a noted water hole for the mob. I considered myself a gangster. That tied me in with armed robbery. The rest were girlfriends, family members, and people who enjoyed being in the company of hoodlums; that were the talk of the neighborhood. The Crystal Room always had a hot band. The best way to conduct business was to move from one bar to the next. You had a face-to-face connection with the guy, and you were able to look into the eyes of your contact. If a captain or an under boss patted you on the back, that's respect. They liked doing business with ex-cons once you were run through the system, did your time, showed some smarts, and did hard time with a smile on your face. Chances are that you would be all right.

It's tough passing yourself off as a standup guy when you are a shell of a man. I was beaten, hung from a pipe, and went to trial. I kept my mouth shut, got twenty years for nothing, and lost my wife and kid. I was ready for anything; life to me was dancing with the devil. At least you knew who you were kissing. I had to tell my sweet baby that I had to go because the cops were after my ass. I told her that as soon as I got set up, I would pick her up. I told her that I loved her, which was not true. It made it easier for me to leave. I already had a girl who was fucked by all. I always said, the more they fuck, the better they get.

Josie was very sexy, and she was well respected by mob members as a standup broad. She was very passionate. I made her brush her teeth till the tube was empty. We went to church, and I told her to confess and tell the priest about all the cocks she had sucked since she was twelve years old. She came out, and we sat together. I felt like we had just gotten married, and she moved in with me. I had an apartment in a high rise that was across the street from a cemetery. I got my binoculars and found my mother's burial spot.

Between stealing cars, buying paper from the totaled cars, and selling alcohol, I was financially sound and able to grab a tab once in a while. My parole officer was happy to see me working. Charlie stopped by the junkyard with a tip. Once in a while he had a payroll score that I liked. I looked around the junkyard, and it wasn't getting any cleaner. I took a ride, and we passed the factory. As they left the factory, we counted the workers. I called the factory and asked about a job and was told they weren't hiring. That's all I needed to know. With that I figured five grand each. That's a year of ball-busting work. I told Gabby keep me on the books as a tow truck driver, in case the parole officer came around. A week later we got off. I gave Gabby five hundred.

Gabby was a year older than me, and as kids we had fun. He wasn't like me. He was business minded and always wanted to get ahead. He had a girlfriend when he was fourteen. He was very handsome. His eyes were light blue, his gaze was intense, and he was quick to anger in the early years. There was so much to do. The girls in the neighborhood were hard to make, and it was a waste of time to talk to them. We both had little extended education. The difference was, he was business minded but never reached his potential. I was definitely a disaster, and when I left the junkyard, he was relieved. He told me that I was a walking time bomb.

He married a woman from a nearby neighborhood. She was stunning, and the two of them were outstanding in appearance. I stopped growing at the age of thirteen, when Gabby started growing. He was a party man. His in-laws were well-to-do, and Gabby fit in well. He would have made a great actor.

I had to make a move. I was running with guys who had to support a family, a girlfriend, and the house. Thank God for their shoplifting wives who were ten times sharper than they were. I was disciplined. I did not smoke or drink. I checked things out, and drugs were out of the question. I could read people like a book, and with ten years in Atlanta, I could spot a screwball a mile away, especially when I was looking into a mirror.

The crew I was working with made the gang that shot themselves look like professionals. On the day of the heist, or on the day we were supposed to be digging a grave, I had to wake them up individually. The driver of the car would fall asleep at the wheel. I was in the front seat steering the car as he fell in and out of consciousness. If I were to divulge his name to ridicule him, I would have to break into jail to get away. The same individual, five minutes after I picked him up, had to take a crap. It was like orchestrating a band of monkeys.

The fuckups were monumental. The Chancy brothers who lived under a bridge in Coney Island and carried a valise with a one-piece bathing suit called me up to join the gang. I knew then if the Chancy brothers could find me, I was in deep crap. I decided to lay low for a while. I still had every nickel I ever robbed. I felt no remorse about kicking in a few bucks to support my kid. My motto was, tough times build character.

The alcohol business was moving along. I put Charlie in on the take. He had a customer in Long Island. I sat in the car and opened the window to adjust the side-view mirror to see what was behind me. A second later, an FBI agent cuffed me to the side-view mirror. I would have been better off if I had used my prick to adjust the side-view mirror. At least I would have gotten a hand job. I was facing ten years on parole violation, plus possession of alcohol. I pleaded not guilty, as usual.

Charlie and I were released pending trial. I was looking at ten years flat, plus the alcohol charge. Charlie was living with his brother. I wanted to postpone so I could get a breather. I knew with certainty that I would have to do a flat eight years, and that's with good time. Six months later, Charlie and I pleaded guilty in federal court to possession of alcohol. We were given three years consecutive to the ten-year parole violation. My full sentence was thirteen years, and we were sent to Lewisburg Penitentiary.

I spent time in the law library, and I soon learned that the court had overturned a case where the litigant was denied his constitutional right to a fair trial. I then wrote to the ACLU and sent them a copy of my case. The ACLU responded and said they would take my case. They also kept me informed. The appeal took around three years, and I was told that my sentence was overturned. I only had a few months left. Lewisburg was a barrel of activity. John Gotti, Angelo Ruggierio, Pauly Vario, Jimmy Hoffa, and Carmine Giganti were there. When I first arrived, I went through the usual steps of orientation and being assigned a job. I worked in the tailor shop. They also had a mattress shop where Jimmy Hoffa worked in a cage by himself. The cage was twenty feet by twenty feet. Jimmy was five-foot-eight in height, and he had a big chest. You could see that he did his job. My observation was only made in passing.

As time went by, I was transferred to the same block as Jimmy Hoffa. Once we came in from the yard, we were allowed to watch TV in the hallway. Charlie and me would be talking about the shows, how fucked up they were, and Jimmy started asking questions. He wanted to know what I thought about this or that. My answer was so graphic that he could not get enough of my responses. If I was in my cell, he would knock on my door and ask me to watch TV with him. He started telling me about the union and about when he first started. The sheriff ran the town, and the sheriff made his own laws. The stories were numerous and interesting.

He had a name for me. He called me Himmler. Jimmy said I had a solution for everything. When the TV program ended, he would put his hand on his heart and salute the flag each and every night. His words were measured. They were never rude or prejudicial. I often wondered how a man with such qualities could interact and manipulate men who had the ability to render you silent with a cold glare of their eyes. I say you must have experience, courage, and the ability to fight fire with fire. Unfortunately you must relax sometimes, and it could be for the last time. Treachery is very patient.

Carmine Giganti was a person who made your blood run cold on a hot day. He loved to play handball, and he loved to play bridge. I, for one, loved to watch Carmine because he was a work of art. He would play handball singles or doubles, and when he got a victim to be his partner, he set the rules. If it's a doubles game and the ball was hit to his left or right and he was not able to get to it, his partner must get it! If not, the wrath of Carmine would rain on his head. You could not bump into him or get in his way. He had never lost a game. The opposition team was not to win, and they were told that if they won by mistake, one of the winners had to say, "Let Carmine play; I twisted my leg."

The bridge game was very funny. He had a guy as his partner who was five-foot-ten and three hundred pounds, and I'm sure the guy knew how to play. The thing was that he never was able to throw a card until he got the okay from Carmine. He held a card in a manner that indicated he was about to throw the card, and Carmine would scream no. He kept flicking the card until Carmine got a peek. The game went on forever. I never saw anyone take a battering like that.

Carmine was eyeballing me once in a while, and I knew one day he would ask me to play as his partner. One day he did, and I said, "I'm not good enough to play with you."

Willie boy, an associate of John Gotti, was good with his hands and a soft-spoken killer. He was respectable. My partner, Henry, told me about an incident when Willie boy was riding with him in a stolen truck, and Henry was armed. The police got behind him, and Willie boy, upon seeing the cops through the side-view mirror, started to panic and wanted to get out of the truck and walk away. The truck in front of Henry stopped, and Willie boy was shaking with fear. Henry told Willie boy to stay put and then opened the door, stepped out, and walked to the truck to tell the guy to move. Henry motioned to the cops to tell the guy to move. As the cop was getting out of his car, the driver of the truck took off. Henry kept talking to the police. The police told Henry to move on.

Willie boy begged Henry not to tell anyone about this incident. He was fearful he would appear weak. That's a big no to a killer's reputation. If Henry passed on the story to others, there would be a great probability that Willie boy would definitely put a bullet in his head. Many times guys who said things that were true and could be verified to others about an individual would cost him his life. The guy who was wrong was liked and had the guy who was righteous killed; I saw it over and over again.

I stood away from the clubs. I never wanted to be connected to organized crime. I did business with them, but to take orders, that's one thing I couldn't do. Willie boy and I walked the yard together, and I talked a lot of bullshit. I had to be a good actor. We were both close to getting out.

He may have been a coward, but he knew how to kill and put a piece of lead in your skull. Willie boy was part Indian and knew he would never be made. Willie boy went to the club on 101st in Queens. I met John Gotti prior to meeting him in Lewisburg. Charlie introduced me to John, who had a nice way about himself. Angelo Ruggierio was an okay guy who could tear you apart with his bare hands. We managed to get along. At that time, I was pulling scores in Brooklyn. I mostly did payroll scores, factories. Everybody dealt in cash. I put Angelo down for a few scores. He kept Johnny informed.

Every time Johnny saw me, he would call me champion. We had many debates. He was an intelligent man, and he treated me with respect. He was no heist man, just a guy with a quick smile. When we met in Lewisburg, a lot of figures of organized crime showed him respect. The boss man kept an eye on John and wrote down the names of those who were able to speak to him. At one time or another we spoke, and I felt we were on the same level. I didn't remember the debate we had, but I soon was pointing out to John where he was wrong on this point or that point. He stopped walking, turned to look me in the face, and said, "Do you know who you're talking to?" There was no smile on his face.

I responded to him, "Do you want me to be a yes man?"

His face lit up and he said, "You crazy little fuck." I called off the debating bullshit.

When I was released, I went to the club to pay my respects to Willie boy and the Gotti brothers. We had a talk, and when I walked over to Willie boy, he passed me a fifty-dollar bill. I took the money, and he asked me to come around any time I wanted to. I was no club man because you had to swallow a lot of shit if you wanted to hang out there.

I went to Henry's place. He had a friend who was called the fox, and he was a cool guy. He was an ace when it came to driving a tractor. Henry and the fox took me to a club where the waitress let you put your finger up her snatch to see how she tasted. Our conversation was crime. If Brooklyn got hit with a nuclear bomb, our conversation would have been, "What do you think we can get for all this fucking junk?"

We hit a few places, and I bumped into a few friends from Atlanta. Most were dope dealers and great guys to know. A lot of these guys were married, had real kids, and lived in homes that were splendid. Some of these men explained how the floor was put together and how much each tile cost, which was a fucking hundred apiece. Most of them were on the heavy side, and their wives were at their beck and call. The FBI waited with patience, fattened them up, and gave them all the rope to hang themselves once the door hit them in the ass and the world crumbled at their feet. They felt faint from fear. The soft life kicks in, and makes you weak and too sick to eat. Racial hate makes you wake up, and the wife and kids don't mean a damn thing. You want out because the fact is, someone might kill you.

I remember the noise from the doors slamming, the ringing of bells, and a hostile look from the blacks and Latinos who couldn't make bail. The FBI dangled sixty years in front of me. It makes you wish you were a dick sucker for a living.

I moved in with the family until I got a spot in Henry's building. I took the studio, and I got a crew who did whatever it took. One of the buildings I had previously lived in had nice furniture in the vestibule. For the rest, they used a credit card. He measured me up for five suits and shoes. I looked like one million bucks. I had a hot car, and I had the world by the balls. What I really needed was a hot girl with a tight pussy.

We decided the best thing was cigarette trucks. They were all over the city. There were several guys dealing in cigarettes, one being Jimmy Burke. I caused an incident in a bar in Queens called The Suite. I knew a few guys out of Atlanta, and they were hanging out. It was Charlie the Jap and Cosmo, who jabs your eyeballs out after he shoots you in the head. He did it in case you pulled a Lazarus and came back to life. Who could blame the guy? That night I made my rounds kissing this guy, and then that guy, always careful not to give the kiss of death to anyone.

One guy was hitting on my girl Josie, whose tits were on his chin. If a girl like Josie falls for a guy, you may end up being a bumper on a Ford. I hit him hard, and he was staggered. He was with a group of guys. The bouncer was all over me. One of Jimmy's managers told me I was one of the luckiest guys in the world. One of the wise guys wanted to kill me on the spot. Charlie the Jap saved my life. He told them I was a bank robber and a standup guy. I was barred from the joint.

I wanted to meet Jimmy Burke. Henry and I went to Roberts Lounge, where an out-of-shape broad was tending bar. I asked for Jimmy, and she wanted to know if he was expecting me. I said no, and she asked us to wait two minutes. Later Tommy Desimone came up the steps, looked me over, ran a look over Henry, and put out his hand. He recognized me from The Suite. We followed him down the stairs to the basement where Jimmy Burke was playing cards. He got up and told me that Charlie the Jap put in a good word for me, and they asked us to sit in. I never play cards unless

I'm playing with marked cards, and even then I generally lose. I started talking shit and had them rolling with laughter. Once I start, the crap that runs through my head could draw out the mind of a heated-up priest. It didn't take much to make the humor-starved individuals take advantage of anyone who might lessen the stress of immediate death.

I, for one, didn't realize the chance I took after depriving Tommy of a kill. His obsession was the need to kill. It was like medicine. I was lucky; I was accepted. The alcohol was flowing, and Jimmy asked us to come around the next day at noon. Henry and I took off. I was fucked up and drunk, and when I got home, I puked my guts up. I really don't like booze.

The next day I met Jimmy at the bar, and we talked about moving cigarettes his way into a forty-foot box truck with a mixed-load fourteen grand. We went to New York and sat on the spot where the trucks came through, and I followed them to Brooklyn. We knew his rounds. I got in front of him and stopped. We got out, and I hopped on the running board, put a hood over his head, and asked for the code number. As he said the code numbers, Henry punched them in.

We were blocking the street, and the horns were blowing. I put him in the car, took off, and pulled to the side to let Henry through. I immediately got behind Henry. When I was sure everything was in order, I took the guy for a ride. One guy shit in his pants, and the stink drove me out of the car. I was able to mimic a black man from my days as a coal man. I told him if he shit again I would shoot him in the ass so he would be able to shit out of two assholes. Three hours later, I took his driver's license and gave him a fifty. Most hijackers give money. I found a spot, walked him to it, and then left. The load was delivered, and Tommy took it to the drop. We got our money, and we paid the car thieves.

I took Josie back to The Suite. I grabbed the tab, and it cost me a grand to be a wise guy. Tommy showed up with his broad. When the crowd saw us together, no one even looked at Josie. I was close to telling Josie to give Charlie the Jap a blow job. I did the next best thing; I told her to run some tongue down his throat. I was very happy things were going well. In this game, things could go from good to bad every half hour.

Henry liked the Fox. I bounced with Tommy at Jimmy Burke's place, and the action was hot and heavy. One night I went over and the Fox introduced me to one of his girlfriends who was named Mary. She was without a doubt the best—an American girl of Italian descent. She had personality and was crazy about the Fox. He was married, and he passed himself off as an Italian. Henry told me that the Fox was Cuban, and I kept it to myself. The only thing I knew was that he was a good wheelman, ballsy, smart, and always laughing

Mary and I became very close. She was five-foot-nine without high heels and a foot taller than me. I always thought the taller the better. She would call me at night and ask me what she should do to get the Fox to fall in love with her. If you could see what he looked like and how charming he was, you would know there was no way he could fall for anyone except himself. It's a natural thing to spread yourself around because it builds up your egotism. It would have been nice if someone could have sprung some nice shit on me. The fact was that a ridiculing fuck like me who was complaining about some asshole broad having an oversized asshole—that didn't fit in with being sensitive.

Mary was an educated and insightful woman. At times I would take her to the Copacabana. I used a Diner's Card that was stolen. The staff knew me. Tommy never paid for anything. Every mob member was in on the act.

At three in the morning, I would take her to the areas in Manhattan that were dangerous. I always carried a gun when I was in that area. These places were infested with prostitutes. She was amazed to see them swarm over the car. Before we entered the zone, I put her bag and jewelry in the trunk of the car. I would drive slow and talk shit with the broads, asking how much they wanted to suck Mary's pussy. I was ready to shoot once they started rocking the car. I took off, and she was mesmerized by the action.

I took her to skid row to see the skids in the dormitory. The dormitory had rooms that were encased in chicken wire, and the doors had padlocks. The men were emaciated and somewhat nude. She was aghast. If she only knew that I had taken quite a number of broads to the cages, and it wasn't cheap. Mary was flipping because a handful of naked mother fuckers stuck their dicks through the chicken wire. The scene was reminiscent of *Les Miserables*. My mother called me miserable all the time.

When I got home, Josie was waiting for me with a Japanese three-bladed knife. I was banging pussy while she was fucking doorknobs. I don't think we were compatible. She was waiting for me armed, so I hit her on the head with an ashtray. She was knocked out, and I took her shit and dumped it down the incinerator. Then I did the decent thing; I called a cab. I got call after call from her. She was mad because I didn't take her to the cages. When I took women to the cages and they got an ovation from seventy emaciated, naked skids applauding, that was their fifteen seconds of fame. Why would anyone want to give that up?

I loved hanging around Jimmy's place. Tommy D had a two-bedroom with a big living room. Guys were coming and going with all kinds of swag. Tommy D moved around in a wheelchair and managed to keep his apartment clean. Most boosters left part of their swag. He sold this and that, and no one said anything. The place was open to anyone, and he had a smile on his face all the time. Jimmy took to Tommy D. He had a carpenter make a ramp so Tommy D could get to the basement. It was a finished basement with lounge chairs, an espresso machine, a huge table, and a refrigerator, packed with cold cuts. Tommy D had found a home.

Everyone loved Tommy D. With his smile, soft voice, and good looks, he could not say no to anyone who needed a place to flop. The wives and girlfriends of the in-crowd stopped off and brought food. The wives loved to hang around and join the banter. They felt safe, like brothers and sisters.

The card game was the thing to see. Jimmy set the tone and tempo of the game. Tommy D, in his wheelchair, sat next to Jimmy, and Jimmy gave Tommy D money to play with. Most of the players were run-of-the-mill, with some knowledge of the game. The rest expected to lose. The big draw was the antics of Jimmy and the crew. There was never a dull moment, and the acting was flawless. It was about the ridicule of an individual who was trying to eke out a meager living without going to prison. Those who hung around managed to get sandwiches from the refrigerator. To run a show, you must have a court jester to take the slings and arrows of the royal court. Those who came knew they would be given a pass and not be ridiculed, but that was providing what Jimmy said or did was not to be challenged. If so, that hair trigger might go off in Jimmy's brain. Jimmy didn't have to be a great player. He had plenty to get him through the night, and most hands were reasonable.

On one night, Tommy D slowly went through his stash. Jimmy would give him more money. Jimmy was coming to a point where he needed to win a good hand to break even. I could feel the energy of the players sitting up in their chairs. One raised, one called, and then one raised. Jimmy called and raised, the others called, and everyone laid down their cards. Jimmy laid his cards face down and mixed them up. No one saw the cards, but he started raking in the money.

One guy said, "Gee whiz, Jimmy, I didn't see the cards."

Jimmy exploded like a hand grenade. Tommy got up, grabbed the guy by the neck, and said, "Are you saying that Jimmy is cheating?"

The guy was coughing up a ham sandwich. He said to Jimmy, "You know I love you, and I would never think that."

Jimmy said, "Go home and fuck your wife." Tommy took the guy's glasses and busted them up with a beer bottle. There should be a play about this crazy shit. I enjoyed being around Jimmy and Tommy.

Pauly Vario was the man you wanted to see if there was a problem. He made sure the boys got their end. I had known the Vario family from the time I was five years old. Paul Vario's father was the superintendent of the school. I remember when I was in the kindergarten, I saw him dressing up as Santa Claus in the hallway. He came into the play room and was giving out small gifts, and when he got to me, I said, "You're not Santa." His name was Pete Vario and he kicked me in the ass many times.

At one time the school principal kept me out of class for weeks. I had to report to her the first thing in the morning inside her office, and she would smack me in the face and tell me to sit in front so she could watch me. I managed to set the paper chute on fire. The fire engines came to the school to put out the fire. Pete Vario knew I was the one who did it, and as I walked through the halls and saw him coming toward me, I bent over, and he kicked me from the side of his shoe. I would actually take off. I was flying, and it was a lot of fun.

The godfathers of my church were businessmen, and they understood the value of respect—not from criminals but from the people of the church. They would make huge donations. They were well known by the parishioners. They weren't flamboyant. My father knew them by name, and some were his customers. They were quiet, but they carried a huge stick. They knew that the average mob associate would never pay up on time. Made men had to make an impression that the money must be paid. Any weakness shown by a made man is an open invitation—not to dinner but to death. Jimmy was a family man, and I never heard that he fucked around with the women. He was watched over by Pauly Vario, and Pauly had rules. All criminals like money, and it leads them to take chances. The lure of money sets them up, and their asses get in hot water. Dopes don't need brains to sell dope!

I was convinced Jimmy was a gangster. He loved guns and violence, and he had no mercy. Giving mercy was a sign of stupidity. The fact is, when someone puts your life in jeopardy and gets away with it, he loses respect for you, and after a little booze, he thinks he can fuck with you, kill your dog, and take your freedom. Jimmy had two sisters who lived above the bar, and Tommy lived next door to the sisters.

I spent a lot of time with Tommy. He was homicidal, but he was quiet, tall, and good looking. I studied him. I knew someday he might feel that my death might give him security. I felt delighted when I could predict that someone's death was imminent. I wasn't happy about the death unless I disliked the person. I would read Tommy's demeanor. It gave me the power to strike first. I knew something was up if the tone of his voice changed. I tried to recall something I might have said to give him the incentive to put a notch on his belt. It's like a fighter knocking out a bunch of bums. It gives him confidence. The more you work, the more you want to kill!

The problem was, these people had friends, and when they were threatened, word got out. A sanctioned hit had to be clean and not enrage the victim's family. The outfit had to warn the family not to retaliate. Any other way is suicide. You could be a cowboy, but not for long. In their mindset, it was him or me.

I never stopped Tommy. I told him, "I'm not a killer, and I don't kill friends."

Killers don't like other killers around anyway. They need guys around them who make them feel safe, and I was good at that. I would make wisecracks, laugh, and push him around like he was my kid brother, hoping it would keep me around for a while. When someone was murdered you could see the tension leave the killer's body like he had a good blow job. After a while, when nobody laughed at my jokes, that didn't make me too secure.

As I was coming and going out of Tommy's apartment, occasionally I would bump into the two elderly women. Their demeanor was correct and proper, and the noise, screams, and gunshots didn't seem to bother them too much. I asked Jimmy about the sisters, and he had a smile on his face as he recounted what the two sisters said. The two ladies, smiling, put a finger in his face and said, "Jimmy, you were a bad boy last night." I never forgot that.

Henry told me he needed money to buy a junkyard and wanted to step up banging out scores. Within a month, we hit two. The next month a driver warned us they were increasing security, and we decided to change boroughs. One of Henry's relatives was running the junkyard into the ground. I told Henry to wise up and dump the yard. Henry needed a tow truck, so he picked up the papers and looked for a heavy duty tow truck. He had a couple of car thieves break into a lot that dealt in tow trucks. He stood by and watched. A fire wagon went by, and one of the firemen spotted Henry and noticed activity going on. He confronted Henry and told him not to move. Henry resisted and was subdued, while the rest got away. Henry was released on his own recognizance.

Anthony got out of prison and rejoined the boys. He was a wild kid, making a lot of moves. I was content to supply Jimmy with an occasional load. Once I took a load of leather jackets to a drop, and the cops were sitting on the spot. I dropped the load and left, but they took my plate number. One thing led to another, and they rounded up a number of us. Fat Tommy and I got a year each in Riker's Island. By the time I served my sentence, Henry was up for trial on the tow truck charge. He put his life in the hands of a judge who found him guilty. The judge again let him out on his own recognizance. Henry had a warrant for another case, but he walked out and skipped town. The FBI was on the lookout for him. The Fox located an apartment in Staten Island for Henry that overlooked the Verrazano Bridge. Henry had one eye and a bad heart valve, and the Fox kept me informed on things.

The feds were good, but they had bad feet. I could smell them a mile away. I would take unusual steps to keep the feds off my back, going back six months while I was doing time in Riker's Island. Henry and the Fox teamed up and were very actively hijacking ninety-foot trailers. Henry was moving cargo and raking in the cash. He had brains and balls. He worked with a network of guys who were reliable and paid on time. He paid his taxes, and the take was a lot less than what he expected. With Jimmy, he bought the load and supplied his pushers. Things moved fast, and everybody was hungry for supplies. Local sweat shops had friends who would buy in bulk, but the demand was huge. Jimmy had an eager force of men who grabbed and pushed the merchandise. Jimmy surrounded himself with men who made you think before you make a move on him. He had his own godfather. He may not have been Italian, but he earned, and earning makes you Italian. Bullshit walks, money talks.

Because of the airport, there was enough for everyone. I was tight with a number of Irish gangsters. I had them looking for someone to take care of Henry. His heart was giving him problems. He had a stash of cash, but the junkyard cost him a ton of money. The Fox got in touch with me and told me Henry had a confrontation with some federal agents. Shots were fired, but Henry managed to disengage himself and escape. The feds were in full force, and the heat was on. I was told by the feds that if I was in his presence, I would be dead.

The feds asked me to give Henry up if I wanted to see him alive. I said, "I have no knowledge as to his whereabouts." I went to Jimmy's place and told him, "The feds must know I'm here most of the time, and I'm going to lay low for a while."

He said, "Fuck the feds."

By hanging around with the thieves, I was able to float around with as many people as possible. That gave the feds a lot of homework. One time the feds dropped in on me while I was balls naked.

I was walking around the room when someone asked, "When are you going to put your clothes on?"

I said, "When you leave." They all got up and left.

I had not heard from my contacts for a while. A couple of months went by, and the Fox came by my place. We walked out the door and did not speak a word. He handed me a phone number, and then we had a few drinks. Two days later, I got a shot at a phone and called Henry. He told me he was in Boston and was living in an apartment in Dorchester just outside the area. He had an apartment with two rooms. The Irish crew introduced Henry to a guy who was to take care of him. They got Henry a new ID and Social Security number. He got food stamps and had his eye examined and treated. Since he had surgery in the bad eye, they wanted to examine it. He was afraid they might have a way of finding out who worked on his eye. He told them not to look into his eye because he was afraid the other eye might go bad. They left it at that. In the meantime, I spent a week with him.

Henry's nurse was a beautiful redhead in her twenties. She got a look at Henry's cock and flipped out. Henry was jail educated. That means that you study on your own. You read philosophy and the things that impress someone. I, for one, studied assholes, to stay alive. Henry spoke softly and got the attention of the ladies, and once he got them in bed, they were done. He was able to fuck a nymphomaniac until she screamed for help. He was in good hands.

I went home and spoke with the Fox. We both felt good for Henry. I said nothing to anyone until a few months later when I bumped into a friend who asked if I wanted to meet a bank robber from Canada. I said yes, and he took me to a high-rise not too far from where I lived. We arrived, and he knocked on the door. Sally stood in front of the peephole and then said, "Ron, I want you to meet a friend of mine."

We entered, and I saw the anger on the faces of the three men who were standing with guns pointed at us. I knew I had made a mistake by not asking more about these men. I put my life in danger by not thinking. Ron, the leader, asked if I was on parole. I said, "No, I have no cases pending, and I'm not on bail."

Ron's problem was, if I had been lying and had cases pending, I could have made a deal with the law, and he would be dead. I tried to reassure him. What helped my case was Sally, who was a well-respected man. He vouched for me personally. Ron knew Sally understood that he and his family would pay. These were very serious people.

I sat down and told him my story, and I knew I was wrong by coming without his permission. Sally wanted to leave, but I told him I would stay. After I got to know Ron, I was sure he would never have sanctioned any meeting. He had an endless supply of bank robbers—the toughest and most dangerous men I had ever met. I told my story and about my fondness for robbing banks. He asked me my age. I had just turned forty-four. I was sure should have been dead by now. The gravity of the situation was compounded with each move I made. For whatever reason, I was not frightened. I looked into his eyes until I saw a smile on his face, and then I turned on the bullshit.

Ron said, "So you want to rob a bank?"

I said, "Yes, when?"

He said, "Tomorrow. You stay. We have it all set up."

There was something about him that I liked. He was a born leader, and he had a strong French accent. The other two spoke some English. We sat around, and I was very excited. He had cognac, but I never liked it and didn't want any. We talked, and he explained what kind of bank we were going to rob and what we were to do. He had hoods for us to wear, and the money was on the counter stacked up. We had aprons to stuff the money into, and we could use both hands. I kept a gun in my pocket. Ron had control of the bank, and we went through the routine a few times.

The next day we had coffee and left for the bank. We had two cars, and we planned to drop one off. We all got into one car and headed for the bank, which was a mile away. We lowered our bodies. Ron said, "There's a cop in front of the bank." He said that he was heading on foot to the bank, which was a block away. As soon as Ron approached the police car, it took off at a high rate of speed. Ron doubled back and jumped into the car. I put the hood on and the gun in my pocket, and we walked in. I said nothing. Ron was instructing the bank employees, and we jumped over the counter. I was on the money and stuffed it into the apron until the money was gone. We went out the door and got into the car. Ron got behind the wheel, and we were on our way. Ron was calm as we jumped into the second car.

When we were a mile from the house, we were still lying low. Then we arrived, at the house. One at a time, we walked to the elevator and the stairs. Ron took the money from the trunk and carried the duffel bag. We relaxed as we dumped all the money on the floor. Each of us had a stack of money in front of us and counted it. If it was close, we pushed it aside. We all recounted the new bundle, and if it was close, that was it. We may have been a little off, but the split was X grand each. Ron had no phone, and he gave me a number to call on a public phone at a specific time. He wanted to see me before he left, and I had to explain to him that my number was bad because of Henry. We set up a meeting at a bar. He told me that the next time he came, he would be with a girl. The girl would come to my house late at night.

I jumped into my car and took a ride to Boston. Henry lived in a black part of town. I told him about the score and gave him ten grand. He had very few expenses. The apartment was paid for mostly by the state, plus he had food stamps. He had a friend from the can who was a hustler and another who had a convenience store in a great area. The area was almost an island, and it was near a beach. The people were mostly Irish and Italian. The people were poor but proud, and they managed. Boston had a way of taking care of its own. Those who wanted to work could find it; those who didn't were able to work the system. There was no need to rob. It was all laid out. It was nice to pick up the check and sit around the house making more babies.

I was a fool not to enter that society. I would've been a lot better off. That little niche of people produced an army of warriors. The girls and boys were indistinguishable, and they were both rough and tough. The warriors were able to roam around and do what they pleased. There was an ice cream factory that was two stories high six feet from the canal. They would climb to the top of the factory, run from one end of the roof, leap across six feet of pavement, and hit the water. It was an awesome sight. The five-year-olds would climb the pilings, get to the top, and jump into the water. The area was isolated and safe. Most of the people sat outside watching each other's kids.

Henry would sit on a bench fucking with the kids, and their mothers would pass by, give us a look, and walk into the convenience store. I would ask them if I could take their kids to the Dairy Queen, and they said yes. Henry and I would load the kids into the car, and that started a stampede of kids going to the Dairy Queen. Half the girls were pregnant, and most lived with their parents. It was one big fuck festival. A little whiskey in the car was all that was needed.

When I walked into their homes, the kids did not want me to leave. I never left without leaving a fifty for the young lady. I told the girls I would be gone soon. I told them I had business in New York City and would be back in a week or two. I was using my car for anybody who gave me a hard on.

I told Henry I had to get back and check a few things out. I also told him John Gotti was asking about him. I told Johnny that I had no word. I knew Willie boy was close to John, and I was a little apprehensive about Willie boy. I got back and went to a garage. The trip set back the odometer six hundred miles. The feds would've loved to find out where I had been.

I was sitting on some hot cash, and I wanted to have some fun with Mary. In the meantime, I had to pass myself around. I was spending time with Tommy D and all the fucks who were hanging around. One was Stacks Edwards, a black man who was in tight with the crew. He was smart and sharp and knew how to keep his mouth shut. Even if we were at the same spot when something went off, and we never discussed the subject openly. If you get a reputation as a loose mouth, that sort of makes you a target if things start falling apart. You could end up with a lot of problems.

I spent a lot of time with Tommy D, who loved to play cards and the fun of seeing someone squirm. The fact that Tommy D was in a wheelchair did not stop him from having a good time. Tommy, Jimmy's right-hand man, and I seemingly got along. He liked the fact that I was much older than him. Most young guys have a chip on their shoulder, but I had a calming effect on him. What drove him crazy was his obsession to kill. Most criminals have family members who were killers, and you had to be careful who you decided to kill. To kill without a sanction gives the stiff a chance for revenge through his family.

Jimmy told me to come down to the card game and sit in. I had a feeling something was up when Tommy D came down the ramp. The game had started, and Jimmy was in a good mood. I only bet if I had a full house, and even then I was insecure about the hand. Tommy was acting crazy and screaming that one of the card players was cheating. Since he was in the company of many, I was sure Tommy wouldn't do anything stupid. Just about then, he pulled out a gun and pointed it at the supposed cheater's belly and warned him again. Tommy said, "Do it one more time and you're dead meat."

Most guys at the table were expecting to see an execution and were shitting in their pants. The guy was in a state of terror. Five hands later, Tommy said, "I've had it," and shot him in the gut. The guy rose out of the chair, and you could see fire coming from the nozzle. There was another shot, and he had the same reaction. The guy was holding his stomach and opened his shirt, expecting to see bullet holes.

Tommy burst out laughing, and everybody was looking at him. It dawned on them that it was some kind of a prank. The jester did not think that it was funny. Everyone else was happy they weren't the jester for the day. Tommy had taken the lead out of the bullets and put wax in the casing. Needless to say, the victim was in no mood to play.

Once Jimmy had handled fireworks on the Fourth of July before I knew him. The bar was jumping, drinks were flowing, and the guys were lighting and throwing firecrackers at each other. The firecrackers were like bombs, and guys were hiding behind cars. Things took a turn for the worse. Shots were fired. Guys on one side of the street were shooting at guys on the other side of the street. Someone yelled that the cops were coming. What started as fun ended up being funnier. The one who told me the story was a cop. Jimmy and the cop were very good friends.

There was another incident at the bar. Four men came in. They were regular-looking guys. I was sitting with Tommy at the bar, and he said, "See that guy who's talking? That's the Iceman." The three who were with him were singers. The guy he called the Iceman told the singers to sing. Only men were hanging around. The three were visibly upset and embarrassed. The fear they showed was sobering. Places like Roberts Lounge drew people like the Iceman. Tommy told me he was the badest of the bad. A couple of years ago, I saw a documentary on TV about the Iceman.

Six months after my last bank job, there was a knock on my door, and a beautiful French Canadian appeared. She told me to come with her to a cab she had waiting. She had her car a few blocks from my house. She took me to Ron's place. I was glad to see him. He was with Claude and someone else who I had never met. Ron had an unlimited number of bank robbers. These men were bonded by blood and fire, and each was capable of taking out a complete bloodline. They had no thoughts of deception or treachery.

This fellow was a farmer who needed a new tractor. I asked Ron if he had ever robbed a bank. Ron said, "Yes, lots of times." The farmer spoke no English, and true to Ron, he had a score lined up. The style of the robbery was the same, except the bank had a guard. The time was set, and the cars were set. Ron opened the door, and I ran to the guard with a gun pointed at his head. Claude took the guard's gun told him not to move. I put my gun in my pocket. Then I used the same procedure as the first robbery. We took the money and went out the door.

The take was somewhat less. No one was hurt. We arrived at the apartment and cut up the cash. This time Ron was here to stay. I told him I was going to visit Henry and made an appointment to call in three weeks.

I took a trip, and Henry got the okay for a new valve for his heart. It was a plastic one, and his eye was responding to medication. I went to a place where we could buy fresh vegetables. Henry knew a guy named Bobby Cool. He was a good-looking guy, and we became friends. He had a sense of humor, plus a good-looking girlfriend.

We were not too far from Southey, a predominately Irish neighborhood. I knew many guys in Southey, most of whom I had met in Atlanta. I wasn't intent on contacting anyone because it was too risky for Henry. There was one girl who was nuts about Henry. The word was out about the size of his prick, and I told the broad's boyfriend to get his bitch off of Henry. Henry's neighbors were having a party, and they invited us to join in the fun. I made sure I picked up some good booze. The women were two to one, and I ended up with the tallest one in the room. She was black as coal and good-looking. Standing up, my face was in her snatch.

The conversation was light, and I told her I wanted to make love to her. We slipped out and went to Henry's place. She was hot to trot, and I slipped it in. It was like I fell into a trench. I told her, "I got the man for you," and she said, "Send him in." I told Henry she was waiting for him. I left the party, and an hour later, he was still waling away. I had my own room, and a half-hour later, she came into my room and said, "You gave me the best gift I ever had."

Henry and I were looking for something to do. We would follow armored trucks to see how much cash they delivered to banks or check locations that had a fast getaway. I was sitting on close to one hundred grand. I could sit back and enjoy the money. I told Henry I had a meeting with Ron and I had to get back. I didn't have any idea what was in store for me. I got back to my apartment and checked out a few strings I had set up to see if anyone had been there, and nothing was disturbed. I decided to look in the swamp for a place to live. I rented a basement apartment and still had my place. I needed to stash my gun and some getaway money. I spent my time hanging out at a marina.

Being around boats was what I needed. I decided to buy a classy boat with a flying bridge, and it cost me twenty-five grand. The boat took me out into open waters and out of the gin joints for a while.

I got a call from Ron. He had another hideout. The feds were checking out calls from Canada to locations, and once they had a pattern, they would check it out. Ron knew that and made a move. He was always one step ahead of them. He gave me an address, and I fixed the time for 3:00 a.m. That gave me time to go from one joint to another.

Nobody went through that trouble to protect Ron. The chess game was hard to win when you played with half the chess pieces. Ron had a dope business and had obligations. He was a mastermind but was losing brain cells. He was leaving fingerprints on me. The problem was, he wanted to hang out with me. The point about danger was valid. It was no good for me and bad for Ron. I told him the feds were across the canal grinding away, and the only thing missing was a monkey.

I hated the dope business. It was one of my nemeses. I was happy to rob you, not make you dopey. Those who sold dope took the fun out of crime, and it was a fucking shame. I liked Ron. He was the first guy I followed and was confident that things would come out right. As for me, I trusted myself to a point. If I came to a fork in the road, no matter if I went left or right, I got a fork in the ass. Ron told me that he had escaped from a Canadian federal prison when he had less than five years to go.

Ron was fearless, and he loved prostitutes. He also took cocaine. He had a homicidal part of him that made you think twice before you gave him any back talk. My whole game was to reason with him when he was in a good mood. The advantage I had was that Ron was sure I was looking out for him. I wanted to protect him from himself. I pointed out the dangers of this or that. I would take him and Claude to places that had no wise guys.

One night we stopped at a joint that had very few customers. I sat at the bar, and Ron turned on the jukebox. The music was playing, and Ron and Claude got up and started dancing and having a good time. I felt a little funny about two guys dancing together. It might give the wrong impression. The bartender made a remark, and thank God the music was loud and they didn't hear it.

I stood in front of the bartender, who was huge, and I said, "If you say that again, either they will kill you or I will. If you think you could kill all three of us, do it now or keep your mouth shut."

He looked down at me and said, "Whatever you want, and it's on the house." He mentioned a few names. I named a few mob bosses, and he apologized. Ron and Claude danced through the night.

I had deprived Ron and Claude of a little fun. I fixed up Ron and Claude with a burned-out slut to pass the time; they kept her for a couple of days. She called me and said they were the sickest fucks she had ever seen. I told her, "That's why I picked you." She said thanks. The broad had the best time of her life.

Ron learned the ins and outs from the prostitutes, and at times he would ask me if I would like to get rid of someone. I looked at him and told him, "Why don't you get some tickets for a hockey game?" The thought made him smile. Ron wanted to know if I wanted someone dead. I said, "Do you want to be with a guy who lets someone else do his dirty work?" He never again asked about any murder.

I've heard many stories over the years about people who bragged about the money they had and then found themselves in a dangerous situation. They get picked up, held, and tortured if the money is in the house. The family gives up the money, and the poor bastard is still murdered. A good friend of mine was shot five times and managed to get off a few shots into the guy. The guy managed to get away without finishing the job. It cost him his life.

I never took a drag on marijuana because I never wanted to dull my thoughts. I needed to be on my toes. Most clowns who got clipped were high on weed or coke. In the old days before forensics, it was dumb. Today it's dumber. Ron had a friend in the Keys who ran some kind of business and was doing well. Ron wanted me to go with him. I said, "He's not going to like seeing you bring guys around. If you remember, you didn't appreciate seeing me walk into your place with Sally."

He thought about that and then said, "You are right."

Ron spent the winter with his girl in the Keys, and it gave me a break from all the running around. I managed to go to the marina. I spent time on the boat before people knew I had one.

A relative of a friend of mine I did business with showed up and asked me to intercede for him in a dispute over money he had coming to him. He ran the story down to me. I told him he had two different families involved. I also said he was right to expect something for freeing a hijacked truck that was stuck with a load of tools. I also said he had to get a made man to act in his defense. Finally I told him not to mention that I gave him advice. He then shot off his mouth to one of the crew who was involved in the hijacking, saying that he was right and he should get a cut of the money. It got back to me that I was out of line. A friend of mine who was a connected guy went to my defense, and the matter was closed.

I was riding around looking for the guy who asked me for advice, and when I spotted him, I told him to jump into the car. I called him a hundred different kinds of cocksucker and motherfucker and started to throw punches. He was young and stronger and was starting to get the best of me. I told Henry to give me a pistol, and he immediately froze up. I let the guy leave.

The guy went to see Willie boy and told him the story. Willie boy then went to John Gotti to get permission to kill me. John called for a sit down in the clubhouse. I went. I knew what was going on, and I knew that John would do the right thing. I walked in and saw Willie boy. I walked over to him and asked what was up. He shrugged his shoulders like he didn't know what was going on. I spotted John and asked him what was up. He told me out loud that the fucking kid was a rat bastard. He pointed at Willie boy and said, "He is going to rat you out one of these days."

I did a lot of things for Johnny and Angelo, and whenever we were together, he would call me champion. I liked him, but I never kissed his ass. He knew every score I pulled. Angelo told him I was the guy who took the lead. John had saved my life. Willie boy wanted to kill me because he knew Henry must have told me he was terrorized. Willie boy faced the last few seconds of his life with a rifle bullet racing to enter his head. The treachery bleeding out of his veins gave meaning to the kiss of death.

I got back to the boat. I had a friend who was the most remarkable man I had ever met. I had to cook him clam sauce and pasta. This man was in his seventies. He was a Jew and looked like George Burns. We were the same size. He always gave me a bottle of whiskey. This man was an old-time gangster, and he would tell me about the old Jewish gangs fighting off the onslaught of Italian and Irish mobs to carve out a niche in organized crime. He was a solo man. I'll never forget him or the man who introduced me to him.

Ron was back in the picture. He changed apartments and was living a little closer to me. He had a friend named Jean who was on the lam. This guy was tough and strong but not strong enough to take on Ron. I was impressed but not fearful. Fear will definitely get you killed. You have to stay loose and follow the next situation with caution. One wrong move can end in disaster.

Ron got his friend an apartment in a nice location. He had no car, and he wanted to get going on a few bank jobs. Ron had some business in Montréal. Claude, Jean, and I rolled around looking to do a bank job. We managed to hit one bank. Then we got back to Jean's place and split up the money. The take was fifteen grand each. I knew things weren't good and the odds were against us. I said we had to take time to find the right one. The feds knew small takes led to more bank jobs.

Jean said he had a girlfriend and wanted to bring her around for drinks. I said right off, "I have no need to meet her," and he said nothing. After that, our relationship took a turn. Jean knew that Ron and I were tight and that he had no cards to play. I still had a strong hand to play. I had a car, and I said, "It's best that I look by myself. The odds are that two men in a car will get attention, but one man by himself will have no heat."

Jean decided to rob a bank with his girlfriend. They were like Bonnie and Clyde. She took the wheel, and he took the bank and the money. She was in a dream world with the man of her life. They were a hot team, and she was ready to hold on to her man. I was glad to get rid of him.

Ron flew in a couple of days later, and he told me that Jean wanted to kill the woman's husband. That sent shock waves. I said, "If he kills that man, it won't be long before we are all in the can."

Ron said, "Let's kick in sixty grand to get him out of the country."

Ron and Jean took a flight to Miami. Ron had a lot of shit going on. The FBI closed in on him. In a one-mile area, they covered all the public phones. I was on my boat listening to the radio when the news came on. There was a short announcement that caught my attention. The report said that Johnny Sutton of Canada was captured. I left the boat immediately and went to my basement apartment in the swamp. I took the guns, the money, and all my clothes and left for Boston. When I arrived, I went to Henry's place and told him the news.

I needed to talk to Sally. He was in the know. I waited a week. I needed to know what was going on. I knew they had nothing on me. I was hooded, and I wasn't into dope. I waited a week and then shot down to Brooklyn and got in touch with Sally. The feds had Ron, who had taken Jean to Miami to flee the United States, and Claude at the Federal House of Detention. I knew the layout at the jail because I had spent time there. I asked Sally how they grabbed Ron. He told me that Claude and Ron outsmarted themselves. Ron was not charged with bank robbery, but Claude was charged with gun possession. Ron had a warrant out for escaping from the prison in Canada, so he was unable to get bond.

We were all masked, and I felt better. In the meantime, I decided to lay low with Henry until I knew that I was in the clear. I had enough money to keep us going. I had money plus pussy. Henry had his operation on his heart, and he had changed. He was a lot slower and seemed disorganized. I took him to the park for walks, and as the days went by, he was able to move a lot better. I kept in shape. I did some running and was thin and strong.

Henry liked the kids of one of his girlfriends. The girlfriend was very young and beautiful, and she had three kids.

I was doing okay. I wasn't interested in any romance that held me down to one girl. There was this one thing that turned me on: fucking in the backseat of a car. And if someone passed by, I didn't care. If a woman is hot, she will fuck on the sidewalk.

Bobby Cool sold us his car, which was in his name. I thought the feds might have a lead on me. Since I was in Ron's company, the good thing was that I knew I had used gloves whenever I was in Ron's apartment. He moved very often, and I was convinced the feds were looking into the drug connection. The bank jobs were done well. Ron was never on my boat, and

I had a good feeling I was in the clear. Nevertheless, as far as New York, I wanted to cool it. Boston was another matter. The place was wide open. The banks were easy, and I was hot to knock one off. I asked Henry about one close by. It was laid out nice. It had a vault, no guard, and one male manager. The rest of the employees were women.

I sat in the car and checked out the tellers, and I made sure I could recognize them all. I bought a female wig, a large-sized bra to distort my figure, a jumpsuit, and oversized glasses. I darkened my face with rouge. The plan was for Henry and me to look like a couple that was waiting for the bank to open.

As the bank personnel were standing by, the manager opened the doors and checked out the bank to see that no one was waiting inside. Then he let the women in. They started walking in, and we were behind them, taking our time. Then we picked up our pace and caught up. One woman turned to me and said that the bank was not open yet. I had to get to the manager before he was able to sound an alarm, and I pushed her in.

Henry was cuffing the tellers, and I told the manager I wanted the money from the vault. I had to convince the manager that I was very dangerous to deal with. This way he would follow my instructions without hesitation. I also told him if anyone should come because of him, I would execute him. In my heart, I knew I would not be able to kill in cold blood.

The manager followed my instructions exactly. I walked him to the vault, and he opened it very quickly. I had a duffel bag, and I started dumping cash into it. I cuffed him to a cart and I told him to stay put until I had left the bank. On the way out, I told Henry, "Let's go." I headed for the Cougar, which was a fast car, and got behind the wheel. I looked back, and Henry was still in the bank. I blew the horn. He came out with keys to open the door of one of the customer's cars.

I jumped out of the Cougar, headed for Henry, and told him we were losing too much time. He got behind the wheel, I got in on the passenger's side, and we took off. We had a car a couple of miles down the road. As we were about to make a turn, I saw a police car heading toward us. We made the turn, and the police were behind us. A fight was about to start as they blew out the rear tire. I told Henry stop the car. He stopped, and we both got out and opened fire on the police. They opened their doors and returned fire. I had two guns and a pocket full of bullets, and I emptied my gun into the police car. Henry stopped a car and yelled for me to come.

I got to the car and opened the door. A woman was sitting in the car, and I yelled, "Why is she in the car?"

He said, "She won't get out."

I looked behind the car, and there were six patrol cars in line looking to see what we were going to do next. I got in, we took off, and the chase was on.

I loaded my gun and Henry's. I shot the back window to pieces, and the cops knew they had a fight on their hands. A police car ran alongside us, and we opened fire on each other. They backed down behind us. We exchanged fire, and spiderwebs appeared on the window. That officer would pull to the side, and another took his place. Each time I shot the window, glass would get in their eyes. The woman who was in the car with us was elderly, and she was looking around at the action and was not frightened. I pushed her head down and told her to keep it down. I didn't want her to get hurt. I was more worried about her than myself.

We entered the town; people were running around. It looked like a festival. A cop was running toward us, right into the front door. I could've killed him but decided to shoot at his feet. He was an easy target but was uninjured. By then I had cooled down somewhat, and I was able to focus. I did not want to kill him, and I knew I was done. I just couldn't give up.

Another cop was in pursuit, and this man was a hero. As I was firing, he was weaving, and I wasn't sure if he was firing back. Nevertheless, he maintained his pursuit. I had never seen such fearlessness. He swerved and then regained control. He put his life back in danger, and this went on a number of times. I didn't see any acts of cowardice on anyone's part. The police were a bunch of tough mothers. We had no way of knowing that a railroad track was about to box us in.

The pursuit and gun firing continued. A police officer was shot, and a number were hurt. We came to a point where we thought that we had lost them. What we didn't know was that a helicopter was directing the squad cars to our position. We pulled into an area where a crew of construction workers was working on a scaffold. I told Henry to pull in. I approached the scaffold, pointed a gun at the construction workers, and told them to give me the keys to one of their cars. They jumped down and ran. I turned around, and Henry was holding the woman. I ran to him and took his grip off the woman's hand. I told her to leave, but she wouldn't. She stood there and looked at me. I glanced at her face, and she showed no emotion.

I turned around and saw a car surrounded by a number of men looking on. I made a run for them with a gun behind my back. They saw me coming and were backing away. I reached and opened the door. I grabbed a guy's hair, pulled him out, jumped in, and took off. I saw Henry with his hands above his head, and I knew I had no chance to help him. I made a run for it.

I made a turn, and in front of me were at least ten police cars that formed a road block. I decided to crash my way through, knowing that there was no way I was going to survive this. As I was riding the center line, closing in on the road block, I noticed to the left of me a string of Christmas trees, and I turned into them at the last second. I hit the trees; they got under the car and raised it up. I was riding on two wheels, and I noticed as I hit the trees that a police officer was actually flying through the air. Another officer who was approaching opened fire. The angle of the car must have protected me. I knew then that there was no God. Any kind of God would have fucked me over. The car righted itself, and I crossed the street and slammed into the train tracks. I lost my gun as I slammed into the steering wheel. My ribs took a hit, and I was listening to the gunshots and the windows breaking.

I was lying on the seat, looking at the skyline, and thinking about how beautiful it was. I heard the sound of footsteps coming closer to the car. I raised my fists, and a cop said, "Move and you die."

I responded, "I'm not guilty."

They pulled me out by my feet and stood me up. A cop came out of nowhere and sucker punched me in the face. He got one more shot at me before the cop said, "Stop, there's a lot of cameras around."

I was cuffed and amazed at the sight of all the police who were standing above me. When I left the road, I went down the slope and hit the railroad tracks. As I was looking up at them, they looked awesome. I felt good that I was able to stand up and fight.

The cop who was in the direct line of fire and continued to pursue me was a hero. I expected to get my ass handed to me. I was roughed up a little, but no damage was done. The woman hostage said in open court that I tried to protect her when I told her to run. She just stood there looking at me and didn't cry. She wanted to see the action. I think I made her day when I said in open court that Evil Knievel had nothing on her.

I was charged with multiple counts of attempted murder, kidnapping, and robbery and was placed in Dedham County Jail, which was built in the 1800s. I was placed in a cell that had twenty-four-hour surveillance and very big windows. We were fed in our cells, and the food was the best I ever ate in jail. I was told that I was in the cell that held Sacco and Vanzetti, who were anarchists in the twenties.

Henry was placed in a cell below me. They let us out for showers and a walk in the yard. The wall was less than ten feet high, and with a little help, I was sure I could bust out. The Fox was telling a few guys he wanted to bust us out. The FBI got that information and notified the prison of the threat. Within a week, a construction crew welded bars across the bars that were in place, and they put lights in my cell. All night long they kept their eyes on me.

I was there to stay, and Mary took a flight down to see me. When she walked in, I knew I had to do everything possible to get out. Such beauty breeds inspiration. I had to get out one way or another, and the way things looked, I would die in jail. We sat and talked, and what we talked about didn't matter. All I knew was that I was inspired! The police sent in word that as far as they were concerned, they didn't have any bad feelings toward us. I felt good. The officer who was shot received the Medal of Valor.

Henry was deteriorating, and within three months, he was sent to a hospital. I was taken to the Federal House of Detention and was placed in the general population, where I was able to talk to Ron and Claude. I told them up front that I would do nothing to jeopardize their freedom. I knew Ron had the manpower to kill and torture the people I loved the most.

I told Ron I was there with the intention to try and escape. I wanted to use the ping pong table to hide under. The new cage was cheap, and it was on top of the building. The building was three stories high. Our recreation area had a ping pong table and a volleyball net. It was a big cage. There were two correctional officers, one on top of the cage and the other in the cage. My only chance of escape was to hide under the pink pong table. I examined the underneath of the table, and it had support beams. I knew that if I was not detected, I would be able to stick my arms and legs into the support beams. I noticed that the cage had a flaw—the screen that covered the top. The metal strip that held the screen down was bent upward. There was an old wooden broom, and if I broke the head off the broom, I could use the handle to stand on. That would give me an opportunity to work on that metal strip. I was able to move it up and down until it snapped, and then I could use that metal strip as a crowbar. Now I had a plan. All I needed was luck.

I talked to Ron, and he told me he had a couple of razor blades. He did not have a screwdriver, but I decided I would take a chance, one way or another. I was set, and it was now or never. I talked to Jimmy Burke, who was in population with me. I was shocked to see him. I told him about my plan, and he told me he would have somebody waiting. He looked at me, and I knew he was skeptical.

I said my good-byes. I went up to the roof at recreation time and stood near the ping pong table. I kept an eye on the screw on top of the cage but made sure I did not make eye contact. The screw in the cage was on his toes, and I had no opportunity to get under the table. The bell rang, and the screw started yelling for everyone to leave the cage. I had to postpone my plan for another day. I went down and talked to Ron. I told him what had happened, and then I talked to Jimmy again. The next day, I went back on the roof, and the situation was the same. It was getting close to leaving the cage, and I got a shot. The screw turned his back, and the screw on top was looking out over the Hudson River. I dove underneath the table. I jammed my elbows into the braces, and I managed to get my legs in. No one noticed me. The screw was having a problem with an inmate who kept shooting the basketball. The screw was behind schedule. He grabbed the inmate, and off they went.

In the meantime, the pain was excruciating. I paid it no mind because I was about to meet Mary again. I waited for the screw who was on top of the cage to drop a ladder, and then I heard him climbing down. There was a gap of five minutes before he opened the door to go down into the control room. I immediately fell to the floor and rolled around to get some blood into my arms and legs. I got up and ran to the net, cut it down, and stuck one end of it through the screen. I picked up the broom and broke off the head. Then I climbed the fence and put the handle through the screen. I stood on the handle and looked at what I had to do. The metal strip was cracked, and I worked it out of the screen. I had the strip in my hand and used it as a pry bar until the screen popped open. I squeezed myself into the hole. It was a tight fit, and I was upside down. I twisted myself and dropped to the outside of the cage. I picked up the net and then had one more obstacle to overcome.

There was a guard shack on top of the roof where a screw was talking to someone. I could see him plainly through the window as I walked nonchalantly to the edge of the roof and looked over the side. The net was only a little over a story high and I knew there was a garage there that was over a story high. I figured I had a free fall of at least a story and a half, but that made no difference. I was going down, and nothing could stop me. I lowered myself onto a steel support for a scaffold. I took a firm grip on the volleyball net and started to lower myself. As I was moving downward, I started to slip. I was holding on with all my strength. I left the net and was in a free fall until I hit the roof.

I knew I had fractured my leg, but my troubles weren't over yet. I still had to jump off the garage. I hobbled to the edge of the garage and hung there for a while. Then I let loose. I wanted to land on my bad leg. I knew I could walk with one bad leg, but with two, I would be finished. I hit the ground. They were doing construction work in the area, and the place was littered with bricks. My face smashed into the ground. I started bleeding profusely, and I knew I was in trouble. I walked to the street. A cab pulled over, and he took one look at me and moved on. I hobbled to a subway station, and there was a Hispanic woman there with her mate. I told her in Spanish that I was attacked and that they beat me and took my money. I asked her for a token, and she looked at her mate. He nodded his head, and she handed over a token. I thanked her and then walked into the station. I went down the steps and into a subway car.

People were looking at me. I was afraid that a subway cop would ask me some questions. I took my sock off of my good foot. I used my spit and the sock to clean my face, with the aid of a young lady who directed me by pointing at her face. I was nervous. The train wasn't moving. I said to someone, "When does the train leave?" He told me they were waiting for the connecting train. The subway car arrived and children poured in.

The pressure was off. I sat there and thought about what I had just done. I knew I had created a miracle. I had a chance again, and I had to leave my life behind. I was on my own. I hobbled down a couple of blocks to a paint shop. In the office, a guy was eating a hero sandwich longer than his arm. He looked at me and said, "What do you want?"

I replied, "I'm a friend of John Gotti's. I need a handout, and if you refuse me, I'll explain to John that you refused to honor his name."

The man reached into his pocket and tossed me a twenty. I asked him to call a cab. The cab took me to a diner, where I made a call. Anthony, who was one of Fat Tommy's brothers and a member of Jimmy Burke's crew, picked me up and took me to an apartment that belonged to a guy who was out of town. The rent was due. I needed a gun and ace bandages. Anthony came back with two guys, the gun, and the bandages. The boys were glad to see me, but I wasn't glad to see them. As bad as I wanted to sleep, I knew I would be in jail when I woke up. My only hope was a woman whose husband was a car thief I did business with. I asked her to pick me up. She said, "I just saw you on TV." I told her to come and get me, and a half-hour later she was there.

I could not get away fast enough. She drove me around until I got my hands on twenty-five grand. The rest was in good hands. I told her not to tell her husband until I was out of town. My leg was killing me, and she got me pain pills. I asked her to drive me to the subway. That way she would have no way of knowing where I was headed. I peeled off a grand and told her to keep it for herself.

That very night I was on my way to Boston. I needed to get Henry out of the hospital. My pain was tolerable. I arrived in Boston. I was sure no one would think I was crazy enough to come back there. I called up a woman named Susan who I had gotten to like a lot. She was married with three children. I called her at her job. She had a car and said she would be leave right away to pick me up. We went to a hotel. I took off my shoe and showed her my ankle. She said it might be fractured. I took a shower, and she put the ace bandage back on the ankle a little tighter. I said, "Stay a while. I need to fuck you right now."

She was the first woman I knew who screamed at the top of her lungs when she was getting fucked. She knew the layout of the hospital because she was visiting Henry regularly. She told me his heart valve was infected and he had high fevers. They had a guard next to him and one outside the door. His leg was cuffed to the bed. I told her, "Go back to work. Then visit Henry and ask him if it's worthwhile for me to get him out." I told her I could hang around for a few days because no one knew that I was there.

The next day she went to visit him and told him I was in town. Henry thought he was in an airplane with the FBI. Susan said, "You will have to carry him with your bad foot."

The situation was bad. I could not do anything. The condition of my foot made it impossible. As bad as I wanted to get him out, I needed a fighting chance. I love life, and I love Henry. The rest is superficial bullshit. I told Susan that I needed her and asked if she would leave her family and go with me. I asked her to go home and think about it. She said, "I don't have to think it over; I'm coming with you."

I told her not to take anything because I had enough money. I also told her to go back and visit Henry. I wanted her to tell him that if he improved and my leg was in good shape, I'd do my best to get him out. We took the car to New Jersey, where I rented an apartment. Susan took a ride to Manhattan to get a birth certificate for me. Susan managed to get the birth certificate under the name Joseph Sansone. Joe was related to me through marriage. When he was a kid, his father was tough on him. As soon as I saw him for the first time, I liked him. Soon after we met, his father died. He was sixteen and loved the fights, and so did I. We would go to Yankee Stadium to see championship fights.

He went with me to Manhattan when I was fucking up real bad. He loved to be in the action. The prostitutes took a liking to Joe. The New York fuck-ups gave Joe a laugh. I made sure he was protected. He got to know Charlie Irish. I got him laid with my girlfriend Rosa. She was hot to fuck Joe because she knew he was a virgin. Joe was fucking Rosa while I was driving. He was riding her like a bronco. It was a fuck show. His mother did not like the idea that Joe was hanging out with me. I knew she was right. Joe was a good kid. He entered the military and made a career of it. He stayed in long enough to retire. I still keep in touch with him. We were always good friends.

I took his birth certificate and used it to apply for a driver's license. I was issued a learner's permit, so I had some form of identification. I told Susan that it was time to blow town. From the place we rented, on a clear day, you could see the Federal House of Detention. I would have loved to have binoculars just to see the guard standing on top of the cage, and him with binoculars watching me with my dick in my girl.

It was time to go to Philadelphia. Susan was very happy because I kept her laughing. I told her how much I loved her. We were inseparable. We arrived in South Philly in the Italian section with the small shops. Everyone was helpful. One shop owner had a son who owned a three-story building. The woman called her son, and he came right down to the store. We met, and he was pleased, especially when Susan smiled. She had dimples that you could fuck. The owner said that the place was a mess, and with my leg, the top of the three-story apartment was a hike. The view was spectacular! I could see the skyline, and it was a thing of beauty. I asked how much, and he said one hundred a month. That was good news, and I said, "I'll take it, and if you decide that you want us to leave, we will give you no trouble." We shook hands that night. We cleaned the stove, and it looked new.

We took a walk to Little Italy. The people were very friendly, and when they heard we just moved in, they gave us the best treatment. So that we would return again that night, we slept in the car. Susan was so happy that she wanted to get fucked in the car. I told her that if a patrol car went by and heard her screaming, for sure I would be back in jail. That night she sucked the foreskin off my cock. God bless her soul. I told her to knock off the Jew boy thing.

We bought whatever it took to put the place in order, and a couple of days later, the owner passed by and was in shock when he saw the stove and how clean the place was. Susan and I fucked our way into the fucking hall of fame. Susan had to get fucked every night, and she put on a display of fireworks that sent the neighbors into frenzy. The screams, the moans, and the pounding of the bed springs turned two lesbians straight. I knew how to hit every button in her snatch. I had schooled her to tell me what she desired, and as she spoke in a freakish tone, I would mimic her words. She became spasmodic, and between my busted foot and my prick, I worked her into frenzy. We were the perfect couple.

On Wolf Street, we would go to all the Italian shops with a shopping bag. I would walk with a cane, and the Italian women were all fascinated with it. They asked if it was real wood. As we walked by, windows would open. Old people sat in their seats with their rosary beads, praying for a smile from me.

I felt like we were succeeding in my quest to live a low-profile life. No one would imagine that a man who pleased his wife each and every night and three times on Sunday to honor the Lord could be a criminal!

Susan and I got jobs working in a restaurant. I started as a preparation man, and she was a waitress. The restaurant was unique. What once was a two-story building was now a restaurant that was over fifty years old. That was in 1974. The food was good, but the cooks were rubber holes. They sucked everything that looked like a cock. The thing was that people were paying for the opera music.

Lois and her husband were the owners. The husband was a fuck. For some funny reason, I never liked husbands, especially if they had pretty wives, and Lois was to die for. That meant that I had to turn control over to mister dick head. Thank God that most women were looking to get fucked anyway, so they would forgive you if you were a little fucked up in the head. You have to take chances to make them hot, like pouring chicken soup over your cock. Once they got a look at your cock, you had it made. It sounds stupid, but there are a lot of girls out there who have low-paying jobs. I advise you to crack down on them, and you will never miss.

The place was packed, and there was a line outside. Lois was the one who got the show going. She had an old-time Victrola that you had to crank. The music came down to the kitchen, which was in the basement, and the sound was getting to me. I felt like I was the phantom in that fucked-up opera house. That feeling was nothing new to me. When things were getting hot, some broad would rise up and sing to some hard on who looked like the midget from Moulin Rouge. The ovation was ponderous, and you would have thought Caruso just finished singing.

Nevertheless, the people were very happy. Most were opera buffs, and they came with their entourages. The place was a hangout for Lena Horne, Tony Bennett, and Pavarotti. Since I was on the lam, I had to keep my head between some broad's legs. Lois had two daughters with the biggest tits imaginable. They were fucking beauties to say the least. At times the daughters wore fishnet blouses. Their nipples would stick through the netting, and the sight reinforced my deviant nature. One of the daughters would be talking to a group of people, displaying every angle in the most provocative way. I loved her self-confidence and her ability to let the ordinary folks look at those wonderful tits. I, for one, never took my eyes off of her.

One of the daughters would come down to the basement to help out once in a while, and my prick would respond in seconds. All I had to say was up scope, and that vicious snake would jump into action. I was there to please her, not to feed her. She would let me perform in my degenerate way. She seemed to enjoy it, but she never let me get too close. I ended up with a bent and broken prick. That gave me nightmares, and I took it out on Susan. She knew me and every move I ever made. I would tell her my thoughts, and she would go insane with passion. The freak in me drew out the freak in her, and all I can say is, we were two freaky mother fuckers.

Lois had a problem holding onto cooks, and it was either that she didn't pay them enough or they were curtailed from displaying their culinary masterpieces. Lois made me the second cook, and that made the first cook go crazy. She fired him and wanted me to take over, and she told me she would give me a hand. She told me the customers were more interested in the entertainment than the food. We would work together for a half-hour or so, and then she had to leave to keep the show on the road.

I really lusted for her. She was twenty years older than me, and she had a wonderful body and a beautiful face. Lois asked me if I would be interested in moving into her home. Her husband had an apartment above the restaurant. I told her yes at least ten times. I also told her she had to tell Susan. She said she already had. Susan was crazy about Lois. We moved in, but Lois wasn't ready to hear the screams reverberate throughout the house. Her home was a mansion, with five fireplaces and all the food you could eat. We had it made. I would meld with Susan in a way that put her into a deeper eroticism.

It was closing in on Christmas, but Susan was sad. I asked her what was wrong, and she started to cry and said that she called her children. I was in mortal danger. I asked her if she wanted to go home, and she said yes, but only for a while, and then she would come back. I asked her if she had been calling from the restaurant, and she said yes, a couple of times. I told her I needed a few days to find a place, and she begged me not to leave. I told her that I just wanted to make sure she was safe. I told her that the feds would question her, but nothing seemed to sink in. I told her go home and stay with the children, and when she was ready to come back, I would be here for her.

I took the car. I went to Baltimore, and an elderly lady rented me a room. Then I drove back. Susan had put me in great jeopardy. I don't know how I didn't get arrested by then. I knew when I asked her to come with me that it was a mistake. To ask someone to abandon her children and then not crack was dumb. I planned on using her and then letting her go home. The thing was, she was perfect. She was hot like burning coal, lovable, and always smiling, never a bitch. How could I let her go? I took my chances.

I still had a chance. All I needed to do was to find a girl with dimples. I was sure there was a bank with my number on it. My life was not over; it was just beginning. I knew I couldn't get emotional. I just had to come up with a plan. The nearest big city was Baltimore. I had to find something fast, and I had to keep the location from Susan. I was sure that once the FBI got their hands on Susan, she would give me up.

Susan and I spoke about the situation. I explained that the FBI would charge her with aiding and abetting. The charge carries a ten-year sentence. When she got back and the FBI got in touch with her, She had to cooperate with them tell them whatever they wanted to hear.

I told her, "They will tell you to go back to Philadelphia and wait to hear from me. The FBI is only interested in me. I need a place to hide out until I find you. You are in my blood. Do your thing with your family. There is a good chance that your husband may not want you around."

I took the car and took off. Then I spent a day looking around. I had to take long enough that she would think I put a lot of time on the road. When I was about to leave, I saw Susan glance at the odometer, and that move forced me to put an added five hundred miles on the car. I used that time to ride around Baltimore, looking around for a location that suited me. The inner harbor was the most beautiful spot. I got a room, and then I headed back to Philadelphia. Susan and I made love for the last time. It was an angry love.

My game now was to get to Baltimore and figure out my next move. The trip was fast. I got to my room, and then I laid there and thought of my situation. I slowly came to the realization that I was free again. The thought that someone had the power to make decisions without discussing them with me first infuriated me. Any feelings I had for Susan disappeared! I knew I had to travel alone and any relationship had to be short and sweet! I heard a knock on my door. The landlady asked if I was going to stay for a while. I looked at her and noticed she looked great for a woman closing in on eighty. I immediately was aroused to such a degree that my hands were shaking. She asked me if I was all right; I had to press my hands against my lap to stop the shaking.

I said, "Okay," in a weak voice.

She told me to rest and then said. "I made some chicken soup. Come down when you feel okay."

The first cardinal law I had made a couple of minutes before was already in jeopardy of being violated. I pulled myself together. Then I rested without sleeping. My mind was poring over her. I had to relieve myself. The shaking stopped. I knocked on her door, and she let me in. I looked around and saw that most of the furniture was old but in mint condition. She had the same point of view as me.

There was a huge park across the street, and it had a skating rink and a soccer field. We ate quietly and talked for a while. I thanked her and then took her hand and kissed it. I let myself out.

The next day I bought her some flowers. She thanked me and then put out her hand. I took it and kissed the palm of her hand and lingered for a while. Then I left. This went on for a month. I knew I had her on the hook when she gave me a gift.

Each week I paid the rent, and we would talk a while. One time she refused the money. I took her in my arms and kissed her, and then I started to undress her. I was so ready for her that I overwhelmed her. Each day as long as I was with her, we had sex with the same intensity. She was drunk with passion, and so was I. I told my lady that I was looking for work. She was a little disappointed, but I made sure that I took care of her each morning before I left the house.

I bought a map of Baltimore and studied it. I had some knowledge of Italian cuisine. I walked from my house to Little Italy. It was a two-mile walk. The area was quite small and surrounded by low-cost housing. The blacks had jobs in the kitchens, and the Italians were the cooks. During the mornings, the crews took over the cleaning jobs. They came in at four in the morning. The preparation cooks did their thing.

The place was lively, everyone was friendly, and the blacks would banter with everyone. The alcoholics would line up, waiting for food to be scraped off the plates. There was a mountain of food. The dish washers took what they wanted, and the rest went to the alcoholics.

I checked out a couple of places. The one I liked the best was Sabatini's. They had the most business and the most celebrities. Before I asked for a job, I befriended a few of the workers. I would hang around with a kid who made heroes. I would fuck with him so bad that he laid on the floor and laugh so hard that he was paralyzed. He begged me to stop. His name was Dan. I often wondered if I could kill him with laughter.

I had Dan to practice on. The poor bastard thought that I was a good guy. What saved him from destruction? I kind of liked him. I asked him, "Do you know of any restaurant that's hiring?"

He said, "Sabatini's."

I got to know one of the owners who was hiring. His name was Giuseppe. When he asked my name, I said Giuseppe. He had a big smile on his face; I flashed my license, and he told me to see the main cook, Renaldo, who also was a part owner. My job was to cook spaghetti. The cook just got off the boat and I only understood a word or two of what he said. I liked him, but I had to learn to read the order when he put the order on the board.

The job was tough. The heat from the stove came from ten pots of boiling water that had to be on the ready for the spaghetti. The handles on the pots were red hot. I had to handle them with my bare hands. After I was done working, the walk back home was dangerous. I carried a gun just in case! My path crossed Senator Mikulski Grocery store. I would stop and flag down a police car just to let him know I had a job working at Sabatini's and I was not some bum walking around. The cop told me that he would keep an eye open for me. He also said, "Get a police whistle and a heavy flashlight." When I got home, I opened the door to my lady and slowly woke her up with my tongue. I still think about her tight pussy.

Each day was the same; the waitress would hit on me. I was amazed that I was not interested. My thoughts were on my lady at home who truly enjoyed the pounding I gave her. At work the word was about Jerry Brown coming to Sabatini's. The Secret Service men had to sweep the restaurant and check all the workers for their ID. My first move was to run, but then I thought it out. I had a legitimate license. I decided that if the Secret Service ran a check on the license, I would just walk out. If he just scanned it with his eyes, I had it made. I had to hold my ground.

I could have taken the day off, but that would have been a bad move. The talk around was that I might be an undercover agent. I was confronted by one of the owners, who asked if I was an agent. I said no. He knew that once I said no, my word would meant nothing in a court of law. I asked him, "Do I have to worry about anything?" He said that everybody liked me and I could stay as long as I wanted.

The fact was that organized crime members frequented the restaurant. It was a must that the mob had to stop over and put on a show for the in-crowd. They walked in with the crew and went through their ritual, with one Mafioso in plain sight at a close distance, brandishing a revolver. You could see the heads turning and looking as the Mob did their thing.

On the day that Jerry Brown waked in, the place was jumping. Two secret service man walked in to the kitchen. One looked at me and said, "How much do you weigh?"

I said, "As much as your two guns." He laughed and patted me on the head.

I kept up with the work. Once in a while, someone would hand me the phone, and a voice would say, "This is the FBI. The place is surrounded." I would respond, "I'll come as soon as I do the dishes."

I was going nowhere. Once people start fucking with you, things start going south. I started thinking about doing a bank job, plus the job was getting to me. Renaldo was giving a pep talk and wanted everyone to pick up the pace. Then he said, "I don't want the broom to hit the floor." At that moment, I threw the broom in the air, and when it hit the floor, Renaldo hit the roof and blasted me for the act. He gave me a good tongue lashing, and as soon as he stopped, I jumped on him. I told him that he was no better than me. I said, "I work, you pay. I give, you give." Then I said, "I quit. I'll stay till you get someone to replace me."

Before I left to go home, Renaldo asked me to stay. I told him that I loved him, and that made him cry. A few days later, I was let go. Now I was a free man. I had some rules that I had to follow, like no bank jobs in Baltimore. I had to leave the state. The jobs had to be no less than a thousand miles away. The FBI is like flies; they can smell blood a thousand miles away.

I had to go to the drawing board. If I took off, what would I do about my lady? I had to take it easy on this one. Losing her was too painful to think about. She was no fool. One mistake and I'd end up in shit city. She was close to the cops; they would come around to check the books. I had to keep her happy. That was no problem. I could not get enough of her. Thank God that Mom Tiny broke me in. Mom taught me every trick in the books. I would have to be a serial killer before she turned me in.

Lady told me that she was German and lived close to a concentration camp as a young woman. She would see young and old march in and never march out. She was so ashamed to admit she was German. She told me not to tell anyone that she was German. I also had a secret—that I was a nut job! I needed money in case I had to flee. I bought a city map and circled the police stations. I found the office of the FBI. I tried to stay clear of the places the law frequented.

The days flew by. No matter how I tried to squeeze a buck, the money disappeared. The only thing that could make me solvent was a bank robbery. If I pulled a bank robbery in Baltimore, for sure I would draw heat. My height was a liability no matter how I disguised myself. I was close to Philadelphia, and I dressed up like a woman on my last bank robbery. I had to get out of town at least a thousand miles; the further I went the better.

New Orleans popped in to my head. I still had a valid driver's license. I had spoken to my lady about my mom having heart problems. When I was ready to leave, I would get the kid, Dan, to call the house. Within a week, I got some of the stuff I needed. I got the kid to call the house. The kid told my lady that my mother had passed away. My lady told me the news as she held me.

I was overcome by lust for her. She could not understand my desire to have sex with her after the news that my mother had passed away. I could not tell her that if I got busted for what I was planning, I would miss the last fuck of my life. I could not let remorse beat me out of the last fuck of my life! I tried to give my lady a month's rent in advance, but she declined. I insisted that she take the month's rent. I told her that I was going to take her apart when I got back.

My plan was to disguise myself as a woman. I had no need to wear a face mask. I needed a wig, dark sunglasses, a turtleneck sweater, and pantyhose to cover my legs. I needed a dent puller to yank the key lock out of a car and a screwdriver to turn the ignition on and off. I took my gun and five grand, and I was ready to make my move. I bought a round-trip ticket to New Orleans. I was able to get on and off the bus. That gave me time to spend time in the city of my choosing.

Before I left, I bought a map of every state from North Carolina to Louisiana. I studied the cities. I was ready, and I was happy. I was alive again. I was going from one emotion to another. It was better than sex. It had been over three years since my last bank robbery. Three years is a long time between jobs, and you can get rusty and make mistakes. But if you have a love for your job, you never lose the touch.

I got close to the Carolinas. I got off the bus. I put my bag into a locker, bought a city map, and checked out the layout. I took a local bus to make rounds. Bank number one no bank guard! My mind set was to hit a small commercial bank that cashed checks. Usually the counter was off to the side of the bank. The money was placed on the counter just before the customers entered the bank. I had a minute or so before the men arrived. Usually people would enter the bank before the main rush. My mind set was to just grab the money and run.

I spent a couple of days in town and picked out a bank that I liked. Then I made some calls to locate a room for rent. I got one, and the landlady came to pick me up. I paid her for two weeks. She took me back to the bus. I told her, "If I'm not back in two weeks, rent the rooms." I needed the room in case something went wrong. I had a place to hide out. I took her phone number.

My next stop was Charleston, South Carolina. The town took me by surprise. It was beautiful. The minute I stepped off the bus, a cop on the beat took a long look at me. I went to the diner and got a newspaper and a cup of coffee. Then I walked back to the bus, and I never got off till I got to Louisiana. Once I got to New Orleans, I got off the bus.

I've been to New Orleans a number of times. The women are either beautiful or ugly. Some had cat eyes the color of Jade. I had to remind myself that I had a job to do. One mistake and I would cry the blues till the day that I die! I had to remember that I was carrying a gun plus five grand. I had to stay off the streets at night and stay away from the hookers. If hooker smelled money, I would be as good as dead. Half of these women were men. They worked you over with a tongue in your mouth and two hands feeling around your balls, digging into your asshole trying to find out where you stashed your money.

New Orleans was a place to have fun. The ones who have fun are the families with the husband, wife, and children. The loners were targets. I got in late and spent the night in the bus station. The next morning, I got a room in a motel, cleaned myself up, and had breakfast in a restaurant across the street from my room. I checked out a convenience store and picked up a local map of the area where I was staying. I found a rail line that was a couple of blocks from where I was. I rode the rail line, looking for an industrial park. As I was leaving the station, I saw a huge industrial park at the next stop. I got off and looked around for a bank.

I must have looked at ten before I saw the one I liked. I did not walk into the bank. I just looked through the window and liked what I saw. Now I had to wait for Wednesday or Friday. They were the paydays. One bank waited until the bank was full of customers. That wasn't good for me. I had to wait for the other, which was on a Friday. I waited until noon. Then she put the money on the counter. The rush started ten minutes later. Things were looking up.

I set it up for the following Friday. I had to steal two cars. I spent less than two minutes in the bank. There was no need to talk. I just had to kick the swinging doors, walk to the counter, and put the money in an apron. I took the gun from my pocket, held it to my side, and walked out. Then I went back to the motel.

After that, I decided to hit a Louisiana Cajun restaurant that had live music. It was infectious. After a few drinks, I asked the biggest guy in the place if I could dance with his wife. He said, "We are here to have a good time." I told the waiter to keep the drinks rolling. I really had a good time.

The next day I went to the train station at an early hour; there were less than ten people standing there. When the train pulled in, they all got on the train. Ten minutes later, cars started pulling in. I saw one car that I liked. I wrote the plate number down, walked close to the driver of the car, and looked at his face. The train left the station. As the next train arrived, I saw what I wanted and took the plate number. I went back to my place and sat around looking at the TV for most of the day. At 4:00 p.m., I was waiting for the owners of the two cars. They showed up at 6:00 p.m. I was sure I had all the time I needed to get the cars and be in Baltimore before the owners got back to the station. I had a few days before I planned to hit the bank.

On the day of the robbery, the cars I picked were easy to steal. I had to place the car one mile from the bank. I had time to get back to the station and steal the second car. That one I took back to my place. I had to walk a couple of blocks to the motel. Time was moving. The first wave of men would hit the bank at noon to cash their checks. The bank employee laid out the money just before noon. I had time to dress up and make it to the bank in time to make the hit.

I was elated with determination. Nothing could stop me now. The money belonged to me. I started to dress for the robbery. I put on my leotards, bra, a wig, a turtleneck sweater, and sunglasses. I also put on an apron to put the cash in. Things were moving very quickly. I arrived at the bank, parked the car, and kept the engine running. I walked up to the window and looked into the bank. I did not see any money on the counter. I was distracted. I saw the reflection of a cop car on the window, and he came to a stop. I opened the door to the bank and turned to him. As I was holding the door open for him, he waved me off.

I entered the bank and walked to the counter that held the deposit slips. The officers enter the bank and said a few words to the cashier. He looked at me and waved. I waved back at him. I was praying he would not come to me. He turned and went out the door. I dropped what I was doing and made a beeline for the door to see if he was gone. He was nowhere in sight.

I turned and saw the cashier put the money on the counter. I almost ran to the swinging doors. I kicked the door, and it flew open. Five steps later, I was on the money. I pushed the money into the apron. Then I turned and took the gun from the apron, held it to my side, and walked out the door. The car's engine was running. I took off like a bat out of hell. I was at the second car in two minutes. I dropped the hot car and took off to the motel. I drove the car to the front door. I had no need to fear because no one saw me switch cars. I opened the door, got my shit together, and took off with the car. Somewhere in Mississippi, I dumped the car. I still did not know how much I had stolen.

The ride home was great. I sat back and relaxed. I was thinking of my lady and that wonderful pussy she had. I needed some loving. At that point in my life, a kangaroo would have done just as well. I got in late and went straight to my room. I stuffed all my stuff under the mattress. I had to see my lady. I opened the door, and she was up and waiting for me. She said, "I thought you would not come back." While she was talking, I was getting undressed. No amount of sex could diminish the passion I had for her. She told me that I was a truthful man, and she believed that I loved her. The truth was her age turned me on.

I opened a savings account and a safe deposit box. I took in enough that it would take care of me for a while. This vault had a combination lock. Anyone with a combination number was able to go in and out all day long. I was very uncomfortable with the situation since I was a crook. I was sure that with some time and planning, cracking those boxes would be child's play. I did not have the time or the inclination to attempt a time-consuming job, taking advantage of a flaw in the banking business.

I enjoyed roaming the city and looking for oddities in odd places. I found myself gravitating to the seamy part of town, where the sights and smells were pungent. I paid two prostitutes to have sex on the sidewalk. Not too far from there was a rundown boat yard squeezed between a factory and a bridge. It had abandoned boats squeezed under the bridge. The rest were rentals. I spoke to the owner of the boat yard. I asked if there was a possibility that I could buy a boat and live aboard on land. He had a number of abandoned boats that looked good but that had no chance of being restored. I spent a number of days going through most of the boats. I made it a hangout. I wanted to see if he and I could get along.

There was one boat that was a thirty-five footer with a wide beam. I was able to stand up straight and have an extra foot of clearance. Bob said, "Cut up and burn a few abandoned boats and the boat is yours." I told him that I needed to hook up the electricity for the chainsaw. He told me to use all the tools I needed to get the job done.

I cleaned out the area next to my boat. I had a plan to learn how to run the travel lift and use the tow boat. I had enough money. I did not need the few dollars he gave the guys who did odd jobs. I did not realize the potential of this yard. No one paid any taxes. When I went home, my lady was glad to see me. She would look at my hands and say, "You look tired." I would look at her and say, "I can't get enough of you." She loved it when I said that to her.

My lady told me something that shocked me to the core. She said, "As a matter of fact, the police were here today going through the books. Some woman was raped, and the police asked about all the men who were in the book and what they looked like. I said that you were quite small. The police told me to get information if you worked or not."

She asked what the rapist looked like, and the officer said the rapist was huge. My desire plummeted; I was in danger. I said nothing. I was happy that I had told her nothing. My best was to carry on as usual and just disappear. Most transients got up and left without a word. I had to do what was right for me. For all I knew, she might be relieved to see me go. Being poked in the ass by a lunatic might not have been so pleasurable. There's and old Italian saying: "Those who walk in circles are nuts!" Blessed be the Lord.

Each day I was able to carry out a few things. As I stepped out of the door for the last time, I had a feeling that I slipped past the law just in a nick of time. I decided to walk to the boat yard. I stopped and had breakfast. I said to myself, "It's a new day. I'm starting a new life. I'm loaded with cash, and I'm on top of the world."

I arrived at the boat yard and climbed the ladder. I was on the deck. My boat faced the open expanse of water. My heart was beating. I was very happy. I was living on the edge, and I loved every moment of it!

Winter was approaching, and a cool wind blowing. Bob, the owner, advised me to get a big space heater and use propane. I bought a small unit to try it out. The boat heated up real fast; I figured it would do the job. It was September. The boat yard kept me busy. I bought a black navy pea coat, a black wool hat, Levis, and black boots. Whenever someone asked what my name was, I would answer, "Sailor."

I found a local diner. I got to know a number of people. I made a conscious decision to be a loudmouth in a nice way. If I hung in a corner, it wouldn't be long before I became paranoid. I had nothing to hide; I conducted myself like anyone else.

I started going to boat auctions. I got a list of boat yards that were going to have an auction on a particular day. Bob gave me permission to use his boat. I used the waterways to get from one boat yard to the next. The boat had twin screws and could pull heavy loads. I became good friends with an auctioneer. The thing I liked about him was that he had a shady side that I got to know. I begged myself not to expose myself in any way.

I soon got hungry for money and was doing small jobs sinking boats and dismantling boats. At the end of the auction, he would tell the boat owner that the boat was missing crucial parts, and he would have to let the boat go at a very low cost. I was rewarded with a sound boat. He once asked if I was ever in jail. I said my father and my brother were retired from the force, and if I got caught stealing, he would never forgive me. I told him that my father died and my brother died in the line of duty. I said, "As for me, I will end up dying in the line of fire."

The auctioneer taught me a lot of useful things, like how to salvage a boat after I had sunk one. The auctioneer was ruthless when he was negotiating. He gave me a lot of play. He once said, "There's something about you that don't ring a bell."

Things were coming to a halt because the weather was real cold. I took over. The pipes had to be shut and drained. They were exposed to the weather. The ones that were living aboard had to cope with the weather. The boats that were in the water had to be watched so they would not sink. Bob made his money doing pump outs.

I was in deep shit, it was freezing in my boat. The little heater was useless. I got Bob to take me to a place that sold space heaters. At first I used five-pound cylinders, and within a couple of days, I had to change the cylinders. One night I ran out of propane and almost froze to death. I hunted around looking for a place that sold one hundred pounds of propane. The cylinders were huge. The guy who sold me the propane had a business on the side selling propane. There is nothing like an honest man who wanted to keep the price down, as if it were the Depression. We did a lot of business throughout the winter. When he saw me coming, his face lit up like his tie was on fire.

I worked like a beaver that winter. There were a number of boats that were listing and had to be pumped out. By noon, I saved the day! I still had to shovel a path to my boat. It was an all-day proposition. Now the boat yard was able to function. Bob was taking in a lot of money from the pump outs. I earned my keep by doing things around the yard. The boat I got from the auctioneer was on land and safe. Bob had a good view from the office, and he kept an eye on me, I made sure I did not beat him for a dime. I applied that old rule, "Don't shit where you eat."

The year was coming to an end. The city was shut down, and the snow was mounting up, but I kept on top of things. No one had to tell me anything. The live-aboard boaters would pat me on the back every time they passed by. I walked to the inner harbor each day, no matter what. The harbor was devoid of snow. Because of the diligence of the city workers, the harbor looked good.

Baltimore was in the midst of a Renaissance. I was very fortunate to view all this beauty! How I handled my life was and always will be a disaster! My motto was, "Die young and be a good-looking corpse." I needed the company of a woman to get through the winter—someone who could take the rigors of a winter confined in a boat that could lead to murder. I had to get a river rat! That type was accustomed to abuse from their fathers and mothers, some were mean and rightly so. My instinct told me that I could tame one and make love like an animal.

Because of the gloomy atmosphere of being enclosed in a small area, a woman would have to be born and bred in a situation that was alien to the average person. These women became half man and half woman. Over the years, they develop an aspect of a caged animal! When I first saw a river rat, she was watching me like I was prey. Most were young. The smell of diesel fuel permeated their skin, and their pussies had a slight taste of low-grade diesel. The friction of the penis rubbing the clitoris could be a safety problem.

To find that type of woman, you had to patrol the waterways to find a boat yard that was in deplorable condition. I used the ploy that I was looking for a boat that was for sale. The weather was still cold, and there were ice floes big enough to sink a small boat. The fathers protected their children from the stranger. It is the same as a tiger protecting his cubs or his kill. If you are the type that gets his kicks by strangling someone to get aroused, by all means enjoy yourself. Mother and Dad and daughter get tangled up every night in bed. To snare this type of prey comes with a great price; she is a sly temptress that seeks revenge on anyone to ease her misery. One wrong move—a slight glance or a tiny smile—and you can be engulfed in flames as you awake from a sleep.

There was a country and western bar across the street from the boat yard. The place was always packed on the weekends. Most were truckers who stopped in to have a beer and relax before they took off on a long run. They needed to shoot the shit with someone. The jukebox was doling out the same bullshit songs. The door opened, and a family walked in and went straight to the tables. I took a look at a young woman who appeared to be at least in her late twenties. She was slim and beautiful.

They were dressed in their work clothes and ordered a round of beer. I felt like someone shot me in the balls. The river rat passed, and I nodded my head. She lowered her head and gave me a smile. The two boys looked at me and asked me if I was a sailor. I said yes. The kids were hanging onto their sister yelling that I was a sailor! The father called me over and asked if I was passing through. I said that I lived across the street in the boat yard. He lit up and said that he had a boat in the yard.

I asked, "What is she called?"

He said, "She's called *My Dream*."

I told him that I pumped it out a couple of days before. I also told him, "I'll keep an eye on it."

I called the bartender and asked if the two boys could have a beer. The bartender said, "As long as they don't drive."

After that we became friends. What I really wanted to do was fuck his daughter with his permission. I was a good disco dancer, and the jukebox had a few good disco songs. I asked his daughter to play a few songs. She was hot to dance. I asked the father if I could dance with his daughter, and he said yes. I then asked her if she would dance with me. She said yes. I had to show her some moves; she picked up the moves real quick and was having a hell of a time.

I made no moves to touch her. I knew that she liked me by the way she looked at me. I played it cool. I asked her when she was coming back. She said, "Tomorrow night."

I said, "I'll be waiting for you."

The father was cool even though he had the face of a spider. He must have had eight eyes zoomed in on me. I asked the father and his wife to get on the dance floor and have some fun. We had a circle going. I started to enjoy myself. I was able to speak to her more freely. I asked her to fall in love with me. She said, "Yes, I want to."

I told her, "When the time is right, I want to make love to you."

She smiled at me.

I said, "I want you to be my woman," and she said yes.

I was excited. We met each week. I just let things happen. I had no way to get to her, and my desire was waning. I spent a lot of time walking to the harbor. Federal hill was a great place to sit and look at the harbor. Federal hill was at least one hundred feet above the inner harbor. The homes were very old. Frances Scott Key's home was there. I would sit and look at the expanse of water that flowed out to sea. The Frances Scott Key Bridge had a tremendous span. I was able to see the office of the FBI.

To walk on the promenade at noon was very risky. A lot of government workers sat there and had their lunch. Walking at that time was like walking into a duck shoot. The nights were when the government workers went home. I emerged and would visit the restaurants that were first class. I had no formal clothes. My wardrobe was mainly T-shirts and Levis. My clothes had to be clean or new. I had to have that clean look. Women would be more inclined to look at you if you had that look. I was thin and in good shape.

Once I was in the restaurant, I would say hello to everyone. This put them at ease, and I was able to make small talk. I got to know quite a number of women that way. Nine out of ten treated me like wallpaper. I was looking for number one if I was going to make progress on the getting laid part. I would pick up the tab, and if I was lucky, I would end up at her place.

The boat yard had the look of desperation. Climbing up the shaking ladder was something to see. Once I gave them a good banging, I was in like Flint. I soon had a reputation. They called me the Buccaneer. They started picking up the tab. I felt like a prostitute, and that put my sex drive into over drive. I loved life, and I loved freaky women.

My problem was to get them up the fucking ladder. If I had someone I liked, I would break into a boat that had some class. I banged those women like they were a bass drum. I needed a dog more than a woman to keep me company. A dog would watch you and try to anticipate your every move. I never found a broad who took one tenth of that kind of interest in me unless I was pointing a gun at her.

I stopped at a store that had some mutts in the window. I walked into the store to see if they had something I liked. The dogs were good, but the price was bad. I said, "Fuck this shit. I'm going to the dog pound for one." I wanted a dog, not a mop. I spotted a retriever who looked at me and said, "You better pick me, you mother fucker!" For a second, I caught an attitude.

I wanted to see if the dog had some fight in him. I had the mutts at each other's throats. The manager came over and said, "Are you nuts? Get the fuck out of here before I call the cops."

I told the cocksucker that I was trying to break up a fight. His eyeballs were rolling around in his head. He said, "Look at them. They're all asleep."

I had to get that mutt! I got Bob to bail the dog out. I said to Bob, "This is a boat yard dog." As soon as I was aboard the boat, he pissed on the boat. I rubbed his face into the holy water.

I decided to get a bike. This way I could get around and have some fun with the dog. The dog was good company. I got a cage for the dog so he was safe from danger. I also got a basket for the bike so I could place him in the basket when we went for a ride.

The boat yard had a little beach. I knew the dog was going to love that beach. I wasn't worried about the dog going into the water. No dog in his right mind would attempt to go into that icy water. I got a small TV and a radio. I loved opera music and classical music. The boat had a high ceiling and a wide beam. The motor was shot and could not be repaired. I took the cylinder head off the motor, put five grand into a glass jar and then into the bore of the engine, and put the cylinder head back on. Then I bolted the cylinder back together. This way I had no reason to go to the bank.

The winter held on like it never wanted to go away. The snow was doing damage to the boats. The ice that surrounded the boats was two feet thick and was crushing the hulls. Once the ice had lost its grip on the boat, the boat would sink. Bob and I would raise the boat, take the boat out of the water, and place it on land to scrapped.

I spent a lot of time trying to keep the boats from sinking. The owners who protected their boats used submerged pumps that circulated the water so it would not turn to ice. Very few had the knowledge or the money to protect their investment. Poor people put their faith in God to do the work for them.

The weather turned warm for a while. My honey and her family showed up. Her father knew I had kept the boat from sinking. That was the first time that her family came down to see the boat. Tom, the father, owned a body shop, and the whole family worked together. They all pitched in to get the job done. I asked Tom if he and his family would like to go to the bar and have some fun. I left the dog on guard.

We arrived at the bar. I asked Tom to leave his money in his pocket and have some fun. I asked Tom if I could do a slow dance with his daughter. He said yes. I then asked Veronica, "Would you like to dance with me?" She smiled, and we danced.

Tom and his wife, Geneva, danced. I kissed Veronica lightly, and the boys screamed as we kissed. I knew that it won't be long before me, the dog, and veronica would be in the sack. I was lusting for Veronica. I thought of a thousand ways of injecting my devious thoughts in to her. The dog always kept an eye on me. At the slightest movement, he was ready to go.

The dog attracted the woman. If I was alone and I passed a remark to a lady, she would smile and move on. With the dog at my side, women would stop and chat. Since I was short and thin, it gave them a sense of security. They could defend themselves against me. When I thought about it, most women were taller than me. I am sure that if I tried anything on a woman of today's stature, I would be overwhelmed, and I would be the one who was getting fucked.

One day I decided to take a walk in the park not far from where I lived before. I still had strong feelings for the landlady. It was a long walk, and I would stop at stores along the way. I was near the park and decided to stop at the ice skating rink and look at the ice skaters doing their thing. It was Saturday morning. The skating rink was an open-air rink. I was watching a number of young girls no more than fifteen years old skating. I walked across the rink with my dog. I had a leash that was ten feet long hooked up to the harness. As I was slipping and sliding, the girls took notice of me and were circling around me.

I made it to the window and rented a pair of skates. I had not skated since I was a kid. I recollected that I was a half-assed skater. Nevertheless, I put the skates on. I had the dog on the leash. I stepped out on the ice, and the blades folded under my feet. I actually was walking on my skates. One of the beauties said my skates were too big. I asked her to help me walk to the office to get a smaller-sized skate. She was falling in love with the dog. She wanted to know the dog's name. She stunned me for a while, and then I said, "Dog."

She said, "I know he's a dog. What is he called?"

I said, "Dog Shit."

She said, "Fuck you, asshole."

I told the guy that the skates were too big, and he gave me a smaller size. I was walking and holding on to the rail. I looked like a drunk. The dog was pulling me along. I was getting the hang of it, so I let loose of the rail. She was laughing, her friends were laughing, and the dog was pulling me toward the girls. I grabbed one of them. I went down and took her along with me. The rest were pulling the two of us up. I was trying to pull a few of them down. The whole crew went down, and we were laughing. I was the last to get up. The dog was pulling with his teeth. I got up and asked if they drank beer. They all shouted out yes! I bought two six packs of beer.

The oldest was fifteen. They wanted to know who I was where I came from. I said my name was Sailor. I told them lived on a boat and my dog's name was Dog Shit. We became good friends. The dog and I came twice a week to visit them after school and stayed until dark to skate at night when it was snowing. It was the most beautiful thing to see. I told the girls as soon as the weather changed for the better I'd be back with my boat to take them to Annapolis to pick up some cadets.

I practiced riding my bike. I got the dog to pull me along. He was getting bigger and stronger as the days went by. He ran along the side of my bike, keeping up with me, and then I would take my feet off the pedals, and he would take over and pull with his harness. Dog was black as coal. He had a red tongue and black eyes. He was beautiful to look at. I gave him red meat, milk, and T-bone steaks. Dog was growing fast.

Spring was in the air. It was like summer. I was dying to get started fixing the boats I got from the auctioneer. I raised the boat with the travel lift and put it in the water. The boat was in good condition, so I had the boat registered. I kept it for fishing and going to the inner harbor. The dog went wild. He loved the open waters. He hopped in and out of the boat. I had a pro teach him how to obey signs.

Life was good, and then someone stole my dog. I felt bad for the dog. He was happy. No one could have had a better life than that dog. I went through a period of rage. I told Bob that I needed time to pull myself together. I took the boat out of the water.

I got in touch with a friend who was able to hook me up with a license and complete ID. He told me that he loved me and wanted me to visit him. As far as money, he said, "Forget about it." He wanted to see me. I said, "I'll be up in a few days."

He gave me a number to use for someone who had no connection whatsoever to him. This guy never had a phone in his house. I took a flight. When I arrived, he was waiting for me. He took me to mutual friend I had known most of my life. He was born in Italy and emigrated to America, and like thousands of Italians, he located himself in East New York in Brooklyn.

This Mafioso was ten years older than me and lived deep in the marsh. As a baby, my mother would take me to the marsh and visit relatives. This Mafioso would play with me, What he considered play was to see how mad he could get me. I was three years old, and he wanted to show me how to fight. He would slap the shit out of me to see if I would cry.

Our friend was a businessman who had connections throughout the world. He never did a day in jail and never was arrested. He had a body guard who drove us around. I met old friends from the penitentiary, and they filled me in on a lot of things that were going on. I met a lot of racketeers from Atlanta. I was told what happened to my partners in crime. I got no good news; most were dead. If you live by the gun, you die by the gun!

They wanted to know what I had done since I escaped from the Federal House of Detention. I ran a lot of bullshit and had them laughing. I kept eating pussy out of the conversation. That was a no-no! As much as I loved them, I knew it was hard for them to keep their mouths shut. I did tell them about the dog. I also told them when they took the dog, any mercy that I had was gone.

I went back to Baltimore with a good set of ID. I still went by the name Sailor. I still had Joe's name on a legal document, and I could use it for minor things. I wasn't sure if Susan told the feds I had a license. I picked up a car that was in good shape but was nondescript. I took a ride to West Virginia and stopped in Charlestown. It was a medium-sized town. I pulled into a mall. It looked like there was a riot going on. Some guys were fighting, and some girls were at each other's throats. I was sitting on the hood of the car when a good-looking blond in her twenties passed by. I shouted out, asking if there was a place that sold liquor. She said, "You talk funny."

I said, "I'm glad I made you laugh. Do you want to suck on some booze?"

She said, "You're kind of little."

I responded, "I'm not kind, but I have a big cock.

She said, "Let's have a drink first."

I said, "I like vodka."

She replied, "That's okay with me."

Just like that, I rented a room in a motel across the street from the mall. As we passed the rooms, each and every person had his door open and was smoking pot or drinking booze. This was a partying town.

Ronda, the girl I was with, was a young and hot female. She was surprised at the length of time I made love to her. Her looks kept me going, I stopped when she said that her muscles were giving out. I opened the door and told her to introduce me to all of the guys. I shook their hands. Ronda said my name was Sailor, and the guys thought I was a sailor. The kids wanted to give me weed, but I needed pussy. They told me to pick one out, so I asked one girl if it was okay with her, and she said yes. Ronda wanted me to take her home first. I said, "I'll be right back."

I did not want to lose Ronda. She was too hot to lose. I took her home and gave her some money. She looked at it and said, "I'm no prostitute."

I told her, "I don't want to lose you. You're the most beautiful woman that I ever met."

She knew I was going to be hanging around for couple of weeks, so she said, "Come by tomorrow. I need to see you."

I went back to the motel. I knew I had hit a gold mine. I pushed the fact that I was a retired sailor. The next night, I had two cases of beer and kept the door open. The women came in and helped themselves to the beer. The best time to fuck was late at night when every female didn't care who was fucking them. The dog was gone, but life goes on. I was walking around in my shorts, stabbing this broad or that one. I was the only one with money, so I set the tone.

Ronda came back that night, and I was glad to see her. I watched her get fucked by someone else. I felt no jealousy. I knew she would be the one who would supply the women. I got to like West Virginia because the people were friendly. Ronda showed me around. She took me to meet her mother, who was a hot chick. We hit it off. This was a new world for me. I had never felt so liberated. The key was money and a lot of balls to act as you pleased. No one will get in your way. I was overly friendly and acted as a father type.

One night Ronda had a date and told me to hang around. I said, "Maybe your mom doesn't like that idea."

Ronda's mother, Brenda, said, "I want you to go out with me to a club tonight. I have a lot of friends."

I told her that I was hot to trot. Brenda told me the place had live music. Brenda introduced me to a few women. The oldest was in her early thirties. I asked one woman to dance with me during a slow dance. I held the woman tight to me, and we kissed. I looked at Brenda. Her man was behind her and was biting her hard on her neck. They were tearing into each other.

Watching Brenda and her partner in action taught me a few things. Drawing blood was not unusual. A vampire thing kept the young girls in a state of lust, Brenda took off with the guy. I took off with a white devil. I took her to the motel, and we bit the hell out of each other. The next day I went to see Ronda. Brenda was sitting in her chair with a bandage wrapped around her neck. She had a smile on her face and asked if I had a good time last night. I said that was the best meal I'd had in a long time.

I was talking to Brenda about how much I liked the state of West Virginia and how I would like to find a place to live there. Brenda said, "If you go to state road fifty, you will find lots of land and the most beautiful scenery you will ever see, and the price is cheap."

I asked her to come with me. Brenda said she had a good job and was not about to run off with a stranger and blow a good job. I said, "I will see you when I get back."

I took my time. The road was good, and the scenery was to die for. I stopped at a small town and had breakfast. The mountains were getting bigger. I still was on state road 50. I slowed down and turned onto a road that was climbing at a steep angle. I came to a plateau. I was in a dream world. The mountain range was awesome. State road 50 vanished. All you could see was an expanse of wilderness. State road 50 cut through and was not seen or heard. State road 50 was a thousand feet below the plateau. The mountain range was not interrupted; all you could see was miles of greenery. It was a sight to behold.

When I arrived, it was dusk, and the stars soon emerged. I was standing on a springboard overlooking a huge quarry. There was a bath house that had hot water. I stepped into paradise. I laid on the springboard and looked up at the sky. I saw the magnificence of the universe with diamonds in the heavens. I knew I had to buy a piece of this animistic soul! I walked down to state road 50 and found a diner that was open.

I walked into the diner. Someone was singing, and the jukebox was blasting away. I sat down and ordered a cup of coffee. I asked a few questions about the area and if there was any property for sale. The waitress said, "There is some on the same road you walked down if you walk back up."

I interrupted her and said, "I have my car parked at the bath house."

She said, "Where your car is, that piece of land is for sale. They're asking four thousand for the property, and it's all set up for a trailer. The people who live there are customers of mine. They will come to you and ask if you need help."

I thanked her for the information and walked back to the car. I needed a shower and undressed. The water was cool. I knew I had to buy the land. The next day I got in touch with the man who owned the land, and we made a deal. He took the four grand, and I had a piece of land for the first time in my life. Like the waitress said, it had an electric pole, a well, and a septic tank. The smart thing to do was just buy a trailer. The dumb thing to do was to buy a house. Most of the homes in the area were trailers. There were two that were cottages, and they blew my mind. They were A-frame houses that were shells. They were built on pilings, and the homes were five feet off the ground. The exterior was complete. The house was picture perfect, like a house in a Christmas postcard. The interior had a loft.

The neighbors came around and asked if I was going to build a house. I was so enthused that I said yes without any thought at all. At first I contemplated leaving the land as it was and getting a trailer. I wanted to keep it a secret just in case I had to run. They knew where I lived; all they had to do was look at the plate.

I spent another night sleeping in my car. The stars were to die for, and the moon was huge. I raised my hand to see if I could touch the moon. The next day, the neighbors came around and offered me a place to sleep. I accepted the offer. I told the couple that when I came back, I would bring a gallon of oysters.

I love the state of West Virginia. If a person had a small income, they would be able to survive. There were no state taxes, no property taxes, and no codes. You could do what you wanted. I wanted to see if I could survive without a home. I bought a barbecue and then looked for the highest spot on the property, which was the road. I parked the car next to the road. I was ten feet from the bath house. I went into town and bought electric wire and some bulbs. I ran the wire to the car, and now I had light. The nights were cool. The lights kept the car warm, and I slept like a baby.

I thanked the couple for letting me share their home with them. I was told that the deer would run through the property. At dusk, the deer waked past my property. They were ten feet from my car. I was seated in my car with the lights off. The sight was awesome. The herd looked so strong, so excited, and so full of life. It was so reminiscent of how I felt when I escaped from prison. The euphoria was mind numbing. To kill something or someone in that state is cruel. People would stop by my property and bring me something. I would pass their homes and offer to help them in any way I could. I decided to leave and come back at a later date. I was anxious to get back. I felt good about the property.

I went straight back to Baltimore. I arrived at the boat yard, and Bob was surprised to see that I had a car. I tried not to answer too many questions. I know from experience that if I was asked the same question a week later, I would give a different answer. I did not talk about West Virginia.

I was hoping that the dog came back, but no dice on that. I did a whole lot of driving around the neighborhood. I was convinced that some kid had gotten a hold of him. Most kids treated dogs like shit. What had me scared was that someone gotten a hold of the dog and sold him to a research clinic. I was afraid they might be experimenting on the dog. I got back to work. People were coming down to check on their boats. Bob's yard was a bullshit yard, but the cost was low. Bob made money because people did not take care of their boats. The batteries went dead, and then the boat took on water. Some boats had to be pumped out once a week, and some had to be taken out of the water. He made a lot of money just starting the boats up.

All the boats had to be winterized. I was thinking of Veronica and how she fit in with me. West Virginia with all that fine pussy was dulling my passion for Veronica. A river rat just did not fit in. Sorry, my dick does all the thinking for me. Veronica and her family came down to the boat yard. I took her aside and told her I was too old for her. She said nothing and walked away as they were leaving. Her dad told me that he was glad I had not taken advantage of her, and he thanked me for that.

A month went by before Veronica spoke to me. Each week I picked up the tab. We danced, but there was no slow dancing; that was out of the question. I made money cleaning hulls and painting bottoms on boats. What I liked best was buying and selling boats. Most people came down and sat around. They barbecued, started the engine, let it run a while, and then left. Those types were first-time buyers. As soon as the weather turned warm, they wanted to buy a boat. They shelled out from two thousand to seven thousand for a secondhand boat. By September, when it was uncomfortable to sit around and they felt a slight change in the weather, out came the for-sale sign taped to the wind shield.

The ones who bought a boat were the ones who were living from paycheck to paycheck. I felt sorry for the guy who wanted to give his wife and children something to make them happy, and for a short time they were happy. The dad, who in a rush, did not take into account the expense of owning a boat. By September, when the weather started to get cold, the boat owners came to the realization that buying a boat was not such a good idea. When it was time to go down to the boat yard and prepare the boat for the winter, at first they both came down and did their best to secure the boat. The wife, who was not too happy to stand around with the wind blowing up her ass, took off and headed for the car. The husband was soon in pursuit of his wife.

A month would pass by, and the boat was in need of a pump out. I would check the battery, and it was dead. Bob would call the owner and give him the news that the boat was taking on water. Bob would hear the wife scream, "Get rid of the fucking boat!"

The guy paid eighteen hundred in April, and I told Bob I'd give him two hundred for the boat. He would carry on, and I said, "Fuck him." A week later, he came down with the title. Then Bob gave him the two hundred. He took off; I took the boat out of the water and winterized it. To leave the boat in the water would be disastrous. The wives were unknowingly working in collusion with me. They had to stop the bleeding of resources. I was there in the nick of time.

I was great at getting a boat in shape. When it came to rot, I was able to dig it out, and with the proper fillers and paint, it would be undetectable. I camouflaged and painted the imperfection, and everything was beautiful. The people I did business with would sell their mothers. I was paying Depression prices with desperate types. Negotiations moved very quickly. I was sitting on a huge amount of cash, so there was no need to rob any banks.

The problem was the thought of robbery kept me riding around, looking for a score. I was an honest man when I had money. I believe I just did it to amuse myself. My boat kept me occupied, especially at night. I filled up the tanks with gas. I would take off and use the flying bridge controls I always made sure the water was calm and the sky was clear. That was the best way to travel. The black sea got blacker as I got deeper in to the Chesapeake Bay. As I left the lights of Baltimore, the stars were brilliant. I was heading for Annapolis, the capitol of Maryland. I kept the boat on a true course. I also kept the speed down. There was no need to rush. I was on my honeymoon with my boat. The city of Annapolis was alive, and the buildings were ancient. The water flowed into the heart of the city. The marinas had the most expensive boats and sailboats. There was no need to plan anything. I just went with the wind.

I sat in a restaurant eating shrimp and drinking beer. I had to join those who were walking along and admiring the artwork that was placed in windows. Most of the artwork was done by the proprietors of the stores. The motif was nautical or anything that related to a ship or a boat. As I walked, I would nod my head as I passed each person. For the most part I was a loner. The years I spent in prison made me mean. I used that meanness to ridicule what I found to be repugnant. Free people are different. If they ran into someone who was repugnant, they would step aside and let him pass, with no need to crush his skull in.

I was very happy looking at this one or that one. I would have loved to have had a camera to take pictures of odd-looking people doing their thing. Then I noticed they were alone, just as I was. The trip back to Baltimore was great. I would sing as loud as I could. I arrived late, went to sleep, and slept like a baby.

One day ran into another. I needed to take a trip to West Virginia. I wanted to find someone to build me a cottage-type house. I took enough money to put a down payment on the house. When I left the boat yard, I had the money plus the five gallons of oysters. The oysters cost me fourteen dollars a gallon. My intentions were only to reciprocate the kindness my neighbors had shown me. I had a big igloo with ice to cover the oysters. When I arrived, I went to the person who invited me to stay at his home. They were overcome when I gave them a gallon of oysters. The others were overcome. With that act, I was the talk of the community. The wives were nuts about me. I asked about a builder, she made a call to the builder, he came down, and we talked and made a deal.

Within a couple of weeks, the cottage was built. The front faced the open expanse. I never saw a better view in my life. I signed the deed in my name. I was able to do it because my name was misspelled and it was never recorded. Plus I never used it on any document. At night it was cool. The house was two thousand feet above sea level. My house was two blocks from the foot of the mountain. The quarry water was cold, and the summers were short.

The closest town was Winchester. I rigged up a stove. I used the bath house to shower and to take a crap. When the snow was four feet deep, I took a shit out the window. From a distance, it looked like tobacco juice running down the exterior wall. I was lucky that no one took a shot at my ass.

The fucking place was a disaster. The electric that was running through the wire was frozen. There was no way to get the house warm. I built a frame in the middle of the house and nailed the thickest plastic I could find to the frame. I went to buy some propane. Everything was sky high, and nobody took a fucking bribe. If you want to ruin a bank roll, go and live with the farmers. I knew I was licked when I tried to get a hard on just to have something to do at twenty-zero. The no jerking off sign came on. The next day the for sale sign was up. I made it back to the boat yard in one piece. It was not long before the phone was ringing, telling us that someone had stolen this thing or that thing. I lost a quick ten grand. I got a taste of my own medicine.

I sat the winter out. I was able to take my bike out and hang around the harbor. There was a crab house a couple of blocks from the aquarium that covered the whole pier. The crab house had been in business since Christ was a kid. One day as I was going to the crab house, I spotted a ship that was tied up to a huge cleat. The ship was the most beautiful thing I had seen in a long time. It was a Launch. There were only six made, all during the Depression. It had a "For Sale" sign on it. I gave the ship a good look over before I entered the crab house. If the price was right and I was able to come up with the money, I could live aboard and pass myself off as a high roller.

I entered the crab house and asked about the ship that was for sale. An oversized waitress said, "Johnny, the guy sitting over there, is the owner of the boat."

I took a look at the fuck, and I knew I had my hands full. I took a few steps and asked if he was the owner of the ship outside. He said yes, so I asked what he wanted for the ship. He said, "I bet you can't pay for my meal."

I said, "My mother and father died on the same day before noon and left me a bundle of cash."

He laughed and said, "Have a seat." He said he had bought the ship when it was new.

I said, "You don't look a day over a hundred."

He said, "During World War II, the *Dana* was high jacked by the US Navy and ran patrols in the Chesapeake Bay. I had Earnest Hemingway on my ship. I could tell a thousand stories." The cock sucker ran a thousand bullshit stories down.

I told the fuck I would be impressed if he told me about the call girls he had on board; then I would give him double the money.

He said, "The bottom line is seventy-five grand."

I said, "Could I go aboard and take a look at it?"

He said, "Don't steal anything."

As I stepped down, I could see the rot on the ship! If the ship took a hit at the water line, it would sink in minute. I wanted the ship, but the price had to come down. With a little help from "God" the price would drop like a rock. I got back to him and said that the ship was in bad shape. He, like a fuck, said, "All you have to do is fill the holes in with cement and a little paint. It will look like new."

I asked him, "Did you ever live in Brooklyn?"

He said, "Fuck no."

I said, "For a minute I thought you might be my father."

The fuck almost fell out of his chair and said, "For that I'll knock off ten grand." Then he wanted to know what my offer was. I said that the price was way out of line. I told him to think about it and cut that price so we could do business. With that, I took off.

After that I would pass the ship when he was asleep and undo the line to the cleat. The ship would drift and hit the post on the opposite side of the slip. He would emerge from below in the nude and sounded the bell to get someone to come to his aid and retie the line. Getting Johnny to lower the price was going to take some time. I had to give him time to recover, and then I would slip in and do a little more damage. I would hang out at the ice rink and keep an eye on Johnny and where he might be. Coming and going on my bike gave me flexibility.

Once I had him under surveillance, and I was able to board the ship take some pieces that were expensive and place the pieces in the bilge. I was always looking for ways to cost him money without causing damage to the ship. I would pass by and talk to Johnny about some kid throwing rocks at the boats that were tied up to the docks in the inner harbor. He would go into a tirade. I became the bearer of bad news.

Johnny had very bad eyesight. At times I would have a conversation with him. He would be standing at the bow of the ship and I would be standing no more than twenty feet from him, and he would not be able to see me clear enough to know who I was. Soon I was playing tricks on him.

When it was dusk, I would bang on the side of the boat to get him to come out and speak to me. He would yell out, "What the fuck do you want?"

I would respond in black idiom, "How much you want for boat?"

He would say, "Get the fuck out of here."

I would say, "I give you fifty dollar. I got money in pocket."

Johnny would scream, "Get the fuck out of here before I call the cops. Fuck you, mother fucker."

I would reply, "I burn your shit boat when you go sleep."

I jammed the shit bowls. He had to take a shit with his ass hanging over the rail and opened fire. The price was dropping but not enough! I had to think long term. I needed to get off big, and this way I could get the ship in shape. If I had an emergency and my freedom was in jeopardy, I had to be able to jump ship and leave immediately. The constitution did not apply to me. I was a miscreant whose only option was to skedaddle when someone knocked on my door. If I was serious about buying a ship, then I needed to come up with some serious money. The fact that the ship was in bad shape was a good thing; it gave me something to do. My main concern now was to put together a plan that was simplistic, short, and sweet.

I talked to Bob about the boat I was contemplating buying. He was enthusiastic because the ship would be a centerpiece for the boat yard. I needed a berth that opened the view to the Patapsco River. Bob had the three berths needed for that. The berths gave me access to go in and out without fear of being blocked in. All these things had to be sorted out before I made my move. The rent was triple what I was already paying, but even with that, it was cheap. The electricity came with the deal. If I had to rent an apartment in the city, the cost would have been ten times as much.

I was set to go. Bob gave me the okay and said, "Take your time." I had my car. That was a good thing because it gave me a lot of latitude; I was able to expedite a plan. I went north. I liked the fact that a lot of people were moving about. It took the heat off me a little.

I wanted a change in way I was going to take over the bank I was planning to rob. The difference was I had to take the bank over completely once everyone in a secure place, which was the restroom. Then all I had to do was take the one who opened the money drop. The money drop took in all the money bags during a three-day holiday. With this bank job, I had to be dressed as a woman. Once I saw that the first employee had arrived, opened the door, and was entering the bank, that was when I planned to take control. That was the premise. Now I had to find the right bank and the right location.

I walked into a number of malls. I wanted an affluent location; all I had to do was to check the parking lot. The cars gave me all the evidence I needed to be assured I had the right bank. I then walked through the mall dressed as women pushing a shopping cart. I had no need to fear any surveillance cameras. I did not look at anyone or speak to anyone. All I saw was that the mall was rolling in money, and my cart was the getaway car. I would pass the bank and see the manager opening the safe and emptying the contents of the safe. It was heartwarming to see all that money.

Now I spent my time checking out a car that fit my needs. I found one at a train station, as usual. To me that was the best spot to pick up a car. On the day of the hit, I checked myself out. I was looking into the mirror. I looked deep into my eyes and saw no fear. I only felt a warm strength to get this over and get my ship! If I died, then so be it.

I had to be at the bank before it opened. I changed the color of the wig. The glasses were the same, and instead of leotards, I put on Levis and a head band that I put around my neck, which I used to cover my mouth and nose. Now I was completely covered.

The car I stole was available at six. I was there when the car's driver departed. My car was a mile or so from the mall. I took the hot car to the mall. I was waiting for the manager to arrive. So I wouldn't arouse suspicion, I pushed the shopping cart around the mall, looking for the manager to arrive with his car. He went directly to the door and opened the door. As he walked in, I was upon him. He felt the barrel of the gun and said, "Don't shoot!"

I immediately said, "I'm here for the money."

I told him to remain with me and usher the women into the restroom as they come in the door. He was all ears. He followed my instructions to the letter. Once the girls were all in, I said, "Open the safe and put the money bags in the cart."

He did so, and I told him to go to the restroom and keep the girls under control. I pushed the cart out the door and walked to the hot car and was on my way. I was surprised that things went so well. I took the cart and the money to a welcome station and disrobed. Five minutes later, I was on my way. I stopped at a motel two hundred miles down the road. I signed in. Then I took a shower and counted the money. It took a while; the take was good, and better than I had expected.

The trip back was euphoric! I was set. There was no need to rob anymore banks. I called my friend. I wanted to meet him, and we set a date. When I arrived, he was there to meet me. I told him about the score and gave him two-thirds of the money. He was amazed; he asked when was I going to retire? I would like to write a book about this guy. He's still alive.

I flew back to Baltimore. Bob was glad to see me. We spoke a little, and then I got back to work. I was thinking it was time to drop in on Johnny. I was loaded with cash. I took the bike, and sure as shit, he was on the boat. The for sale sign was still plastered on the side of the hull.

I yelled up to him, "Did you get any bids for the ship?"

He wanted to know if I was still interested in buying. I yelled, "If the price is right."

He said, "If you have any money, I'll take thirty grand cash!"

I said, "Too much."

He screamed, "Give me an offer."

I said, "Not till you are reasonable."

A week later I cut the line. Then I took off and laid low for a while. A few days later, I passed by and told Johnny that a gang of black kids were throwing rocks at me as I was passing the inner harbor. Johnny was salivating. I had him by the balls. I told Johnny, "Come down, and you got a meal on me!"

He came down, and we walked into the crab house. I showed him five grand for a deposit on the boat. I wrote down a number. He looked at it and said, "Twenty-five." I went to seventeen, he went to twenty-three, and I went to twenty. Johnny said, "Done deal." Then we shook hands." I told him that he was responsible for the ship until it was in my berth. He signed the title. I signed the title, and then I gave him the five grand.

That same day he had a captain who took the ship to the marina. I went along for the ride. To me it was the *Queen Mary*. I put the title in the safety deposit box, along with the money I had stashed in the box. I paid Johnny with the money I had just stolen.

I did not know the power I had. I could marry someone. I could be a preacher man. I could also be a respectable man. Hallelujah. The ship sat in a spot that attracted people who drove their cars over the bridge. At a distance the ship was majestic where it sat. It was perfect. At low tide the ship made a cradle that kept it from listing. Now I had a job. I was self-employed; this ship was in need of major work.

I got a guy who did surveys on boats and was knowledgeable about most anything pertaining to boats. He did a lot of work at the marina. His name was Don. We became good friends. I asked him to survey my ship. He took on the task, and after two days of grueling work, he gave me a list of what had to be done, plus the material plus the labor. He told me that the cost was close to thirty thousand dollars. I had a plan. I wanted to do the work myself. Don was busy, but he said that he would show me the right way to do things. Don had the knowledge, and I had the brawn. I told Don thanks.

I had a map of the city of Baltimore. I circled most of the marinas I had not visited before. I was looking for marinas that were big and did work on wooden boats. I stopped at several boat yards before I was able to find one that was working on a wooden boat and doing a job on a hull. I hit the jackpot. Not only did they do work on the hull, but they also sold the planks I needed for my ship. I was dealing with a foreman who had control over everything in that yard. I told him I had just bought an eighty-foot yacht, and I told him the location where the ship had been docked for months. He knew the ship, and he knew Johnny. He asked if I knew anything about wood work. I said I did not! He then advised me not to start and to get a professional. He said, "I saw that hull and for anyone to walk in this yard without any experience, he is just kidding himself."

I asked him, "Would you mind if I work for you for nothing?"

He said, "The yard policy is that everyone must be insured and be paid. I'll tell you something—for a little guy, you got balls. We open at eight in the morning. Get here before the gate is closed, and then sit on that slip and watch what the shipwright is doing."

Within a week I had the shipwrights laughing their asses off. After a while they would ask me if I was a Mafioso. I would tell them I was kicked out of the mob because when I gave the kiss of death, they claimed that I lingered too long. One guy took a liking for me and built a gig for me. The gig was important because the planks had to be bent properly so it would fit the curvature of the hull.

Things were moving along at a fast pace. I felt that I knew enough to be on my own. I ordered the planking, the screws, and a number of other things that would be needed to do the job. I told the foreman where I lived. I wanted to know his opinion on the job once I had finished. The gig was a gift from shipwright. I had to rent a steamer to bend the planks. I had a raft that belonged to the yard.

The first thing I did was to start on the water line. I did this when the tide was low and the river was calm. I ripped out the rotted planks, inserted straight planks, and screwed them in. I was surprised on how good it looked. When I came to the bow, it had a curvature that was acute. I was lucky that the rot was a couple of feet above the water line. I turned on the steamer and placed the plank in to a tube. Once the steamer was up to pressure, I opened the valve, and it did not take too long before the plank was ready to go into the gig. I was able to bend it to the right curvature, and it fit in perfectly. The rest was a lot of hard work, which I enjoyed tremendously.

Inside the hull some of the ribs were in bad shape. Don gave me a hand on what to do. He showed me how to sister a new plank against the rotted wood. What I did was extremely important to the ship. I spent over a year working from morning to night. I was so passionate about what I was doing. I left the engine to Don to take care of; that was one thing that had to be done by a mechanic.

Bob was proud to have the ship in his yard. People who were driving over the bridge were coming into the boat yard to see the ship. Most wanted to come aboard to see the interior of the ship. I told them that the ship was under renovation. Thank God for thievery. Even God needed a five-finger discount. The deck was leaking badly and had to be sealed from above. The decks where all teak, and it was beautiful. The salon needed work on the roof. It had a few small leaks, so I put fiberglass on three separate roofs and stopped all the leaks.

The ship had three pumps that were in good shape. I was able to leave and stay a week or so away. Don told me that he would check the ship each day. I decided to go to West Virginia to visit Ronda. She was surprised to see me. I did not tell her I had bought a huge boat. I wanted to surprise her. I was hoping I could talk her into coming with me to Baltimore. She took me to a spot to have some fun, which we did. I talked about a small boat, and she was interested to see it. I said, "Let's go." She wanted to pick up a few things, and she told her mom she was going to spend some time with me. We took off. The ride was nice, and she was doing the driving. I was thinking about fucking the shit out of her.

When I pulled into the boat yard, she saw the ship and let out a scream. The interior of the ship was not finished. It needed to be painted. I left that for last. The main thing was the salon, and it was looking good. Ronda loved the salon. I asked Ronda if she would like to take a walk to the inner harbor. There were so many activities going on. I was sure she would have a good time. Ronda was young, beautiful, and full of vigor. We walked and talked and took in all the sights.

We decided to go to little Italy and have some lunch at Sabatini's. I wanted to visit some old friends. I believed that she never ate any Italian food except pizza. Renaldo walked over, hugged me, and was truly happy to see me, as I was as happy to see him. He looked at Ronda and said, "Did he kidnap you?" I told him she was my grandchild. I did not want him to know that she was my girlfriend.

Later she asked me, "Why did you say I was your grandchild?"

I told her, "I did not want you to be ashamed because of the age difference."

She said, "Don't ever do that again. I'm proud to be with you. I love you just the way you are."

After that I loved her as a daughter and a lover. I could not wait until I got back and could do a number on her. We walked, we talked, and when we got back, we fucked and fucked. She wanted to take the ship out for a ride. I had to disappoint her. I still needed time to learn how to handle the ship controls. It still was risky to go out without someone who knew how to handle the ship. I said once I got the ship certified we would take a trip to Annapolis for sure. I had taken the ship out with Don. He knew how to handle the ship in any emergency.

I was not ready to handle that size of a ship on my own. The controls were operated by compressed air, and the engine room had two diesel engines. The fuel tank could take on 750 gallons of diesel. The generator with a converter was able to take AC and change it to DC. The ship had fifteen batteries. I was dazzled by the enormity of the equipment on display. I was charged with a rage of happiness. I must needed to turn intimidation into submission. I was the master. If the ship failed to respond to my commands, I would sink it. With time and acuity, I would master the controls. The ship was tight, and with good seas and low winds, I was able to make the necessary adjustments to keep the ship on an even keel.

My papers were in order. The ship had a compass and charts that were three by four feet that showed the way to Florida. The ship drank fuel, and when it dropped to five hundred gallons, I got in touch with the boat that delivered fuel. I had the man who was delivering the fuel pump out the old fuel and then put fresh diesel in the tank. It was costly, but it was the right thing to do.

Ronda was in no hurry to go home. There was one incident that took place while Ronda and I were watching TV. I heard someone jump on the ship. I reached under the bed and got a gun. I could hear footsteps as he was heading aft, and I waited for the intruder to open the door! As the door swung open, he walked in holding something. At this point common sense said, "Don't pull the trigger." I was focused on his hand. He was clutching a can of beer. He dropped the beer and raised his hands without any command from me.

I asked, "What you are doing on my ship?"

He said, "I was just looking around. I thought that no one was aboard."

I said, "I could have shot you. I don't want to call the police because I believe you. I want you to promise me that you will not come back."

He said, "Okay."

I marched him out the back door and said, "Keep walking and don't turn around."

Ronda was surprised that I had a gun and was ready to use it. I told her that there were a lot of people who stole parts from boats, and they understood one thing that would impress them, and that was a gun. The yard was safe; there were a number of people who were living aboard their boats, and all of them had firearms. The boat yard was not a first-class yard. Bob ran the yard with the least expense. Once a yard made improvements, the costs of the improvements were passed on to the renter. Bob had the wisdom to let things remain as they were. He could see that people were struggling to come up with the money each year.

Bob's health was not very good. He depended on the tenants to keep the place clean. I was always on the lookout for broken boards. That was very important; someone could injure themselves seriously on a broken board. I was telling Ronda that if I got the ship certified from the Coast Guard, we could make runs up and down the inter-coastal river, as far down as Florida. I could get groups of people of the same persuasion, with the same likes and dislikes. I could create an itinerary from Baltimore to Florida. Could I achieve all this and not be detected? I needed a crew of young girls willing to do the right thing.

My devious mind was running at top speed and closing in at the speed of light. The possibilities were injuring the head of my penis. I was planning to enter an operation that had complications that would rise to the level of lunacy. To navigate the inter-coastal waterways is a task of heroic magnitude. The first order of the day was to go to the Coast Guard office that was in the vicinity of the FBI. With my sailor outfit and my blond beauty, I was ready to take on the world.

We went into the government building and started talking shit to the sailors of the Coast Guard. None heard a word I said. They had their eyes on Ronda; I could see the look she had on her face. Most were over six foot tall and really good looking. I was standing next to them; I must have looked like a garbage can. Nevertheless, I made myself known when I yelled to them, "Attention" a number of times before they turned their heads toward me. I had a folder with a picture of the ship. They looked and looked with deep interest.

One young man said, "Do you own this ship?"

I said, "Yes I do! That ship was in the waters of the Chesapeake Bay."

The picture of the ship was in an eight by ten taken when she was in the possession of the US Coast Guard. The men looked like they had found their long lost grandmother. I said, "This young thing is my first mate."

That was the beginning of great love affair. I asked questions about the possibilities and if I would be able to secure an authorization to run charters to the state of Florida. I told them that the ship was less than a mile from there. That very day six of the young men came down to the boat yard and asked to come aboard. I told them, "Permission granted." With that, they were all over the boat. I told them there was beer in the refrigerator and to help themselves.

I asked, "Which one of you wants to take the ship out for a ride?"

Ken let be known that he was there as a friend and not an agent of the Coast Guard! He also added, "Whatever I do is between me and you."

I told him, "Let's shake hands on that."

He said, "I'll let you know if you have a shot."

He took the ship out, and we were on our way. Once we passed the Frances Scott Key Bridge, he asked one of his friends to take the wheel as he went down into the engine room to check out the engines; he was down in the engine room for over an hour. He came up and told me that the engines were fine, but the engine that ran the compressor was in poor condition, and it had to be replaced. He also said we should not go any further. Ken said, "If the engine goes, the compressor will stop, and we will be at the mercy of the wind."

Ken told me not to spend money in the hopes of getting a certification. He told me that the US Coast Guard is very stringent and it was almost impossible to get certified without spending tens of thousands of dollars. I thanked him for his assessment.

Ken navigated the ship back to the marina and spent the rest of the day surveying the ship. He gave me a list of things that must be done. Ken took the job. The cost of labor and material was close to three thousand dollars; Ken refused to accept any money.

That night Ronda and I took the small boat and headed to Annapolis. It was a slow ride; we were sitting in the flying bridge. Ronda was so beautiful; I asked her about Ken. She looked me in the eyes and told me that she was in love with Ken. I told Ronda that I loved her but I wouldn't stand in her way. I asked her not to feel sorry for me. I also said that things could remain the same between us. I said to Ronda that she and Ken could come aboard without any invitation.

I said, "I don't want to lose you. I want you to be happy, and I will respect your relationship with Ken."

We arrived in Annapolis, and we walked we talked and we ate. That night the water was choppy, so we spent the night in Annapolis. At daybreak we had breakfast and then headed back to Baltimore. That morning she called Ken and said, "I told Sailor that I was in love with you. We are always welcome to come aboard. Sailor said he wants to throw a party on the ship in a couple of weeks, and he wants me to come up with a few girls to have some fun."

I felt relieved that Ken came to my rescue. Nothing is better than fresh pussy. The ship was looking good; my focus was on the ship. The wind was a factor. The ship was like a sail. If I caught a twenty-mile-an-hour wind, that could be a problem! But with Ken aboard, he was a master at the controls. Things can change quick, especially when returning to a narrow channel. If a boat is coming and a boat is going in a narrow channel at high winds, the captain must be experienced to handle a ship that is eighty feet long on a weekend when there were a multitude of boats in the water. Ken knew his stuff.

Dom the mechanic would take me out during the weekdays and put me through a routine. Nevertheless, there were those who loved to jump the waves and would cross the bow of the ship. That was dangerous. A speed boat at high speed could sink the ship in a matter of seconds, and there was nothing I could do. I did not want to involve Ken or his crew, but Ken had a few of his buddies who were on patrol and got to know my boat real well.

Once I was in the Chesapeake Bay, I put the ship through a rigorous routine. I worked the twin engines as much as I could. I put one engine going aft and the other going forward. I was able to make tight turns. If I had a problem and someone was hurt due to negligence on my part, I would have to take off and run for my life. The Coast Guard took pride in an investigation, especially if the ship was documented.

I spent a lot of time working on the interior of the ship. I wanted it ready; I paneled the walls with mahogany. Ronda called me and said she had four girls coming down. She got Ken to get a few guys who were sailors. The way I looked at it, I could grab some pussy here and some pussy there. I had the boat with the diesel fuel come to the marina and fill up the tanks. I had a lot of food on board and a shitload of beer. Whisky was a must to loosen up the girls. As for myself, I never was a guy who was hard up for whisky.

On the day of the party, we left the marina. The forecast was for calm seas and hot weather; the ship's upper rear deck was twenty-seven feet long and eighteen feet wide. The rear deck had a roof to keep the sun and the rain out plus a four-foot deck that was two feet lower and was closer to the water line. The lower deck had a stainless steel ladder that enabled someone to lower him or herself into the water. The music was blasting away. I told the guys and girls to get to know each other. The guys were starting to loosen up, and the girls were nuts about the sailors.

I had the controls as we passed Fort McHenry we went under the Frances Scott Key Bridge and we were in the open waters of the Chesapeake Bay. The boats honked their horns in respect. Everyone was circling around the boat. I was so proud to be the captain and owner of the ship.

I asked Ken to take the helm. We planned to go to Annapolis, but the girls wanted to go swimming. We dropped anchor, and the ship settled down. There were no waves. I had rope that floated on the water and was a safety measure. I told the girls to stay close to the ship. I climbed to the top of the boat and jumped into the water. It was great fun. Everyone was climbing and jumping into the water. I took off my underwear and was waving my prick at the girls. They took off their bras, and their tits were floating in the water. I had a semi-hard on, and I was handing out beers to the guys and girls. They were kissing and drinking beer.

One by one they went down the stairs to the rooms. Some fucked in the bathtub; Ronda was switching and fucking all the guys. Ken got the message and was in his glory. When they were fucked out, I was still banging away. I saved Ronda for last. I asked her if she was happy, and she said yes. I told her that Ken was watching her sucking pussy and cock.

She said, "Those hard pricks turned me on."

We spent the night anchored. I never had so much fun in my life. Ronda knew that she and Ken were not a twosome anymore. I told her, "The way Ken was looking at you sucking cock and pussy, I got feeling that you turned him into a freak. If you want him and you love him, I am sure you got him by the balls!"

Ronda stood with me for a long time. I never told her my story. She once asked me if I was ever married and if I ever had children. I said, "Not that I know of."

Ken still was coming around. I liked the kid. A lot at times he came with a good-looking woman and we would talk. I taught Ronda how to handle the smaller boat. We fished together in the night with the stars shining in the heavens. I liked the way we treated each other. Yet she still loved Ken. I told Ken, "Ronda still loves you, and you would be remiss if you let her slide by. Just think, when you have been married for a while and she is still bringing fresh pussy home, what better deal you could get? I bet you won't complain about that."

Ken thought about that and said, "Sailor, you are crazy, but you are right."

We left it at that. Ken told me that the charts I had were outdated and needed to be replaced. Ken took care of that, and I appreciated the work he put into it. With all the work going on tearing down the old piers, it caused a lot of old pilings to float around in the Chesapeake Bay. The pilings were like crocodiles submerged and were ready to strike with enough force to punch a hole and sink a boat. I told everyone that if we were unable to get back to the marina before dark, I would have to pull into the nearest port. Luckily I had never had to spend the night anchored or in port.

The weather was changing; September had arrived. I spent a lot of money on the ship and diesel fuel, but it was worth it. I never had so much fun. The arrival of a new day was like a gift from God. I loved the girls, and the girls loved me, as long as they were having fun. I did not expect any women to love me if I was a deadbeat.

The deeper the winter, the cheaper the boats. I needed to buy some boats. It was Christmastime, and people needed to buy Christmas gifts. A sentimental asshole would let his boat sink before he let his kids go without a Christmas gift. I went to marinas that were close by. The owners gave me the keys to a boat to look it over because they knew me, and I did a lot of business with them. I would ask the owner of the boat yard if the boat was in good shape or if the owner of the boat was desperate for money. The owner of the boat yard had a reason to give me the info. The simple fact was, whatever money the boat owner got, he had to pay the owner of the yard whatever bills he owed, which was substantial. I had no need to steal any parts. All I had to do was pick up five boats a year at the right price and then sell them in the spring.

There was one guy who was living on a boat in the marina. His wife had him kicked out of the house and also his dog, which was an English pug. I knew him for a number of years. Everyone liked him. He would sit in his boat and speak with anyone who passed by, or he would walk from boat to boat and say a few words to this one or that one. He was an excellent conversationalist, and there were others who would be able to express themselves adequately. I sat in my boat and listened to the conversation, which I enjoyed. It took me back to the years I spent in prison. There were inmates who would discuss topics and use words that flowed with a fluency of music.

He was a good man who had the misfortune of getting cancer, which developed very quickly. Once he was convinced he was going to die, he took it like a man and carried on as usual. He did his own shopping. One day he went shopping with his dog, left his dog in the car, and did what he had to do. He walked out the door and was in shock when he was not greeted by the dog. He made it back to the boat yard and kept saying, "Someone took my dog." He stopped eating and did not open the door.

Bob called the man's wife and told the woman her husband was despondent and would not open the door. Bob said, "She just hung up."

I asked Bob, "Should I break the door open?"

He said, "No, let him die in peace."

He soon died, and I rendered the boat useless. A week later the wife came down with her boyfriend. The boyfriend took the key and tried to start the engine, but there was no response. Bob gave the wife a bill for two thousand dollars. I loved the look on her face when I told her that her husband busted up the boat. She said, "That's the kind of fuck that he was," and she turned and walked away.

The winter was upon us. I was lucky that a drainage pipe ran from the factory next to my ship; the water was hot and kept ice from forming. Boats that were left in the water with nothing to protect them boat were crushed by the ice, The ice was three feet thick and crushed hulls. They remained so until the ice would melt. Some had pumps that were under water and circulated the water, which kept ice from forming and crushing their boats.

I used the winter to work on my ship exclusively. I put a lot of money and time into the interior of the ship. I finally understood that the originality of the ship must be kept to maintain her dignity. Speculators and people with money knew the value of originally. I believed I would live out my life on the ship and die an old man aboard my ship.

Ronda and the winter did not mix too well. There was danger of living on board when the boat yard was encased in ice. A couple of beers were all that was needed to fall off the pier and send someone to an untimely death. Her decision to leave was the right thing to do. It was not right to keep a young lady in conditions that could only lead to a deplorable ending; I made sure that would not happen. I let her know that she needed to go home and be with her family and friends. I took her to West Virginia. We had a little to say to each other. When she got out of the car, I knew that our chances were slim to regain the passion. I still had hope that with a little ingenuity and depravity, I could and I would conquer her! was a little dejected, but it dissipated. I still was a free man.

The Patapsco was frozen solid, and the view was beautiful. The ice breakers would crush the ice on their way to the power plant to deliver fuel. The swans landed and sat there till they tried to get in flight. It was a struggle for life. The dogs knew that they had fresh meat and slowly walked on the ice toward the swans. The swans would flap their wings as hard as they could, but to no avail. It was a slaughter! The dogs remained till they killed all of the swans. I was thinking I could have helped the swans, but I would have had to fight off a pack of dogs that were starving; I had no business interfering in a righteous kill, especially when I was able to go to the supermarket and buy whatever color swan I wanted.

At night I would spend the time in a bar across the highway. I got to know most of the truckers. Most were very quiet, and I would tell them a lot of bullshit stories. Some of them opened up and would answer whatever

I asked them. I had a love for guns, and they had guns for sale. Some had stuff from each load; my problem was that I could not afford to get arrested for anything. I had connections for any merchandize, but the thing was I would not last a hot second. I just knew that I had to behave myself and stop acting like a common thief. I had money; the thing was, I got used to having a woman around that I cared for.

I started to get a little paranoid. Just to being was not enough to make me happy. I realized that I still had to pay a price. I had to do some hard time and get angry again. Just being secure and having money was not the answer. I needed to be driven like an animal with the hate beaten out of me.

I met a guy at the bar, and he was a singer who sounded like Elvis Presley. As soon as he stopped singing, I bought him and his wife a drink, and we soon became good friends. He asked me where I lived. I pointed to the other side of the highway. He smiled and wanted to see the boat I lived in. We walked across the highway. I took him to the boat that I first lived in. He was amazed, looked at me, and asked me, "How can you live in that boat?"

I laugh and pointed to the ship. His mouth fell open, and he said, "I see that boat every day as I go to work."

I asked him and his wife to come aboard and look around. He looked at me in a different light. I showed him around. They were so comfortable that she asked me if they could stay the night. I was more than happy to have them spend the night on board. The ship was in good shape, and the interior was done. The heat from the radiator kept the boat warm and comfortable. The next morning we had breakfast, and they took off. Every other day Bill and his wife would stop by, and he always had a six pack of beer. I showed Bill the boat that I had on land, and I told him as soon as the weather warmed up we could do a little fishing.

The months flew by. The weather warmed up, and the boat yard was humming. I put the boats together, and they looked good. As soon as the person saw the boat, he had to have it. I felt a lot better. As long as I was working, I had no time to think about anything. I did not want to fuck up my thought process. I was making money, and I was good at what I did. I was buying and selling. I would take a down payment for what I paid for the boat plus the material. This way I got my money back.

I went to a lawyer, and he made a contract that the people buying boats from me would pay me a couple of hundred a month. This way I always had money coming in. If the guy fell on bad times, I told the fuck to forget about it. I had his wife sign the contract. It was more or less a scare tactic. I had no intention of dragging the guy into court and getting myself locked up. I wanted to keep them as friends. Those who did not make a move to pay, I just took the boat back and resold it to someone else.

I had five boats paying two hundred a month. That was a lot of money in the '80s. Ronda was back with Ken, and we had a lot of fun with the small boat running back and forth to Annapolis. Ronda told me that she wanted to get married. I told her that if she was to be married and wanted a righteous life and a husband for life, she had to get rid of me because I was a bad influence. She said, "I don't care. I want you at my wedding."

I said, "I'll be there."

She set the date for couple of months later. I drove up to West Virginia and stayed with her mom. The wedding took place in her mother's home. Ronda and Ken looked great together. I put ten grand in an envelope and whispered to her that there was ten grand in the envelope and ten more if she let me fuck her with her wedding dress on. She looked at me and smiled and said she just might take me up on that! I was thinking that was not a normal thing to say to a bride. I never was accused of being normal. Anyway, the government wants everybody to be normal so they pay their taxes on time.

Some knew that I carried a gun. I did not allow anyone to take a picture of me, and I never allowed myself to fall in love. I never got angry if one of my women was kissing a trucker. There was a lot of "no" in my life. I was paying the price of being an outlaw. My dream was to die in a hail of bullets. I had no family or legitimate friends to speak of; I was surrounded by a ring of people who would sell me out in a second if they had any idea that I was wanted dead or alive!

When I started to feel sorry for myself, like I'm doing now, I just thought of the times when I was locked up with an animal, and all I could think about was how to kill the fuck in a thousand different ways with one wrong move for killing a worthless asshole and ending up doing time for the rest of my life. I doubted if someone could provoke me. I would placate myself by thinking of revenge. With revenge you can put it off to another time. That was your way out. There was no need to kill him right away; his time would come. Each and every day when I arose, I would yell, "I fucked them for another day."

I had a plan. I needed to get away, a fresh start with new faces. I needed to do whatever it took to con myself. It's easy to lay in bed and paint a picture of a beautiful life ahead. I wanted to get a RV, travel around the country, and buy some land in Mexico. I was able to speak Spanish enough to make myself understood. If I put all my money together, I had enough to keep me solvent for quite some time.

I was taking the ship out on a run, just to keep it from running down. I put the ship up for sale in a nautical paper that distributed the ads across the United States and overseas. I started getting calls from everywhere. Most of the people who were interested wanted to know if the ship still had its originality. Most knew each item and wanted to know if it was still on board. I was truthful because I did not want anyone coming from out of state and accusing me of being deceitful. Several people told me that my ship in its state of originality and with all its accessories intact was worth one hundred thousand dollars. In mint condition, it was priceless.

I was in shock. I had one person come to see the ship. This man, upon seeing the ship, was in awe. He looked at the ship like it was the most beautiful thing he had ever seen. I wanted out, and he wanted the ship. We made a deal. He asked me to stay aboard till his crew arrived. He told me that it would be reborn again. Two weeks later, he returned with his crew, who were very professional, and took the ship out to see how it performed in the open waters. Much to their surprise, the ship was ready to make the move and be on their way.

I looked as the *Dana* made her way up the Patapsco river toward the Chesapeake Bay. This was the first time that I had seen the *Dana* at a distance. I still had my smaller boat and a place to stay. All I wanted was a suitcase in case I had to run for it. I still went to the boat yard. I kept doing what I had been doing.

Suddenly I started to cough. I became very ill. The sweat was running down my face. I knew I was in trouble. I asked Don to take me to the hospital. The hospital was within eyesight. Don drove me to the hospital and walked me in to the emergency room. I knew they would make me die if I sat down. I lowed myself to the floor, and someone said, "Put him on the gurney."

I was conscious when they put me on the gurney. One of the doctors started to yell that I was having a heart attack. There were six of them around me, all yelling that I was losing my kidneys. The doctors got me to the ICU. They stabilized me. One nurse wanted my Social Security number, I knew that if I gave her a number, they would get into my life history. The ID that I had was as if I was born yesterday. In that case, the hospital would notify the police department that I was a John Doe. Lucky for me I was carrying five thousand dollars in cash in my pocket. The rest was in my safe deposit box. The doctor told the nurse to leave me alone.

I stayed in ICU for a week and then spent a week in recovery. When it came time for me to leave, I was told to go to the office to pay the bill. I walked into the office, and the person in charge gave me a bill for ten grand, plus the bill for the doctor who gave me X-rays. She then handed me the five grand. I counted off fifty bucks and told the nurse, "I will pay the hospital fifty bucks a week."

She said, "Give me your Social Security number and you don't have to pay anything at all."

I told her that I didn't want anyone to pay my bills. She looked at me with such disdain that I actually felt ashamed of myself. I gave the doctor two thousand dollars so I could continue to be treated by him. I sat it out for a few months. Each week I gave the hospital fifty and the doctor fifty.

I did a lot of walking. I was getting stronger and was ready to go back to work. Don had a job to do on a sixty-foot boat, and he wanted me to work with him repairing a hull that had a number of broken ribs. He told me that I did such a good job on my ship and this was an opportunity to get a little more experience as a shipwright. I needed a tool, and I asked Bob if I could use a tool that was in the shed.

Bob said, "Take what you want. By the way, an FBI agent was in my office an hour ago looking for a guy who had a boat in my yard and showed me a picture of the guy."

It was one of my customers who was wanted for rape in a number of cases. I asked him a few more questions, and then I was assured that I was in the clear. The next morning as I was working on the hull, I heard someone yell, "This is the FBI."

I turned, and two FBI agents walked up to me and said, "We believe that you may by a fugitive."

I continued working and said that they had the wrong guy. I was looking dead into his eyes and said, "Is that the guy that you want?"

He said yes, and he gave me the picture.

I looked at it and said, "You don't think that is me, do you?"

He said, "He resembles you."

I had a file in my back pocket, and I was ready to commit suicide. I was sizing up the two of them. I could get one but not two. The one in front of me was saying, "Let's go to the car. It appears it may not be you."

He asked me to get off the scaffold. He took the file from my pocket, and we walked to the car. One agent got in the back, and the other was behind the wheel of the car. He asked me what my name was. I said Howard Hense. I took out an ID and a birth certificate. I had a perfect ID. He asked me what my mother's last name was. I said Lillian Miles. He let out a laugh and said, "He doesn't know his mother's name."

I said, "I think you are trying to bust my balls. Fuck you." Then I opened the door and moved to get out. The FBI agent whose name was X grabbed my hair, pulled me back into the car, dug his fingers into my throat, and told me, "If you keep it up, I'll rip it out."

I said, "Fuck you."

I was hoping that if I was able to get away from the car, they would have the right to kill me. I could have done something when I was standing on the scaffold. As I thought about the files that were in my back pocket, there was no way that I would have done anything to injure the agent. There was a third agent who jumped on me. He had a rope that he wrapped around me from head to foot. I looked like a salami. I knew what was in store for me: life in prison without parole.

The trip to FBI headquarters was full of threats. I was going to sue for false arrest. Then I was shown my wanted for escape poster. Then I admitted that I was Michael Castello. I was taken to the Baltimore City jail. I was placed in population and permitted to go to the mess hall. All the inmates were looking at me; I was the celebrity of the week. People who lived in the marina were interviewed.

I was soon called to the federal courthouse to be extradited to the state of Massachusetts. The federal agents were there, and a number of people from the boat yard where there looking at me in disbelief. The prosecutor, in a loud voice, was reading a litany of charges. The judge asked if I was guilty of assault on the two agents, and I said, "Not guilty." Then I asked the judge if I could approach the agent. He nodded his head. I took two steps toward the agent, put my arms around him, held him for a while, and then released him. I asked the judge, "Was that violence, Your Honor, or an act of love? Your Honor, you be the judge."

The judge was smiling and asked if I wanted bail. I said, "May I be the judge?"

He said yes, and then I said, "Denied."

Agent told the judge that I was the toughest man he had ever met. I was very proud of that statement. I was extradited to the new Federal House of Detention. I was the only man who escaped from the old Federal House of Detention without help. I was a fugitive for eleven years.

I was given a lawyer. The judge, a black woman, wanted to know how I escaped from the prison. I was about to answer the judge, and then the lawyer said, "Don't answer that question." She smiled at me. I was picked up by the marshals and taken to Dedham County Jail in Massachusetts. I was surprised that no one in the legal department remembered the case. That was good news for me.

My lawyer got most of the charges dropped, and I was given twenty years to serve. With good time, I could be out in ten years. All I had to do was to become invisible. There is no place to hide. I became an ostrich. I buried my face into math and Spanish. I studied the dictionary.

It was very difficult to be a loner. What helped me was my case was the violence and the gun duel. My lawyer gave me a stack of documents. I was a virtual lunatic, and they left me alone. I did not want to be in any gang.

I entered Walpole State Prison. I was assigned to a block that evaluated the inmates. Once you were evaluated, either you remained or you went to a lesser-security prison. Because I escaped a maximum security prison and because of the severity of the charges, I was to remain in Walpole.

I was given a single cell. The bed was concrete. The fact that I was alone boosted my feelings. When I got to Walpole, there was a war going on among the prisoners. At first I washed myself in the cell when I saw that it was dangerous to be alone.

I decided to sit with the Irish crew. They had their own table. If someone sat down and he was not Irish, they would pick up your food and throw your tray into the garbage can. If you came back again, you had to be crazy or one tough bastard. I had a tray and sat down as they were coming in to the mess hall. One kid said, "Get out of my fucking seat."

I told him, "It's my seat now."

He turned to his friend and said, "This fucking *wop* wants a fucking beating."

I popped up and said, "I sat with the Irish crew in Atlanta," and then I named a dozen guys who were killed in the Irish war.

When he heard that, he walked over to a guy who was in his late sixties, and they spoke. The kid came back and said, "The old man wants to talk to you."

With that I walked over to his table, and he said, "Have a seat. Tell me what you're here for."

I ran the story down about the bank job, the shootout, the escape, and being a fugitive. I told him that I was mostly a gangster, not a racketeer. I named a guy he had to know. He said, "My wife is coming to visit me today. Go back to your seat. Nobody is going to fuck with you."

With that, Walpole was a great place to have a nightmare. Stabbings were something that people did to show someone that they were not to be fucked with. I was in good shape. I did not have to prove to anyone that I was someone to be respected.

Walpole was an insane asylum. Once a guy went to take a shower, and someone set his cell on fire. The smoke was black and the fire was a dark red and orange. It was so evil looking that it scared the shit out of you. I thought that Atlanta penitentiary was a bad place to do time. Walpole made Atlanta look like a country club. You didn't go crying to the screw there. If he didn't like you, he had a way of spreading the word that you were a rat.

Walpole had a reputation for the most murders in one month. Suicide was the leading killer; death was a way to escape the pressure of someone who had control over your life. The bell was ringing, the place was on lockdown, and the screws were kicking the shit out of someone. There were inmates who enjoyed the brutality of the beatings. I saw a guy being carried by his hands and feet. Blood was flowing from his head, yet he had a smile on his face.

I was assigned to the hospital. The hospital was a small cell block that housed the craziest prisoners who were wearing restrains and had the use of one hand to eat and wipe their asses. This was the place where they sent the guys who challenged the screws to a fight. The screws loved it. When someone fucked with them, the screw got to like the screwball, after beating the fuck half to death. He would come by and ask the guy how he felt and then open the door and give the guy a smoke.

At first I did my job mopping the floors. Then an inmate took a piss through the bars to infuriate me. I could not retaliate against them. That act was a minor thing. If I retaliated, they would hold a grudge and try to set you up with a handful of shit into your face. They always had shit in the bowl, and they let you know that they would use it. There was a fine line that I had to walk. They would ask me to do something for them that was reasonable. If I said no, I was on the shit list, and it could be dangerous. They could be ingenious and come up with a weapon that the inmate who brought up the food would bring to take out your eye, no matter how the screw shook down the cart. They managed to bring one piece at a time to construct a weapon that was able to blind you.

Most of these guys would never get out, and their mission was to injure you for life. That would make them very happy. I wasn't trying to make them miserable, but they feasted on hate. Those are the ones who, if they were allowed to enter society, would be like hungry beasts. They would devour whatever came their way. Word was out that I was a bank robber and I took on the cops. This made them look at me through a different prism.

The blacks and the whites were at each other's throats. Racial hate was prevalent. Nothing could change that. Basketball was a catalyst that drove each side to try and kill each other on sight. The Celtics would win the title, and the blacks went nuts. I hated basketball! Then the schools decided to bus kids to other schools, and that reinforced the anger. Integration had to be done. Things today are a far cry from yesteryear. The blood and the tears have brought us together.

The winters were brutal. Nevertheless, the yard remained open for those who wanted to walk around. At times the screw and I would pass each other, and he would smile at me because he loved to walk on the coldest days. I never passed up the opportunity to go to the yard no matter what.

One day when I left the yard and walked into the block, someone was laughing and yelling that the space shuttle had exploded and all the astronauts were killed. I was so angry with this guy that I could have taken him apart and never put the pieces back together again.

Then I was transferred. Norfolk looked like a college. Every cell had a window, and it was a good place to do time if you had the right friends. The prison had four baseball fields, handball courts, and a brand-new gym. The inmates were civil and were glad to get along. It had factories, and if you waited your turn, you had the opportunity to start your own business. There were some who made furniture. Most were leather shops, and some made hand-carved jewelry boxes. I made a lot of friends and a lot of enemies.

I had a friend who was a straight guy who had his own business and was a very wealthy man. We were the same age, and we came from the same neighborhood in Brooklyn. We were in the US Marines at the same time, but our paths had not crossed until we met in the county jail in Dedham, Massachusetts. He made a decision to go to trial on a homicide. I advised him not to go to trial. I told him to take the deal for five years, but Andy wanted to be exonerated. Andy did twenty years and was paroled and violated his parole. I lost touch with him. There is a possibility that he may still be in jail.

I went to work in the tailor shop; it kept me busy, and the time was flying by. I passed out one day, and I was taken to the hospital. They ran some tests, and the doctor said, "Continue with the medication," which was an aspirin. The doctor knew I was in bad shape and did nothing. I kept walking, and I was lifting weights. I knew that there was a connection between me coughing and my heart. I had a feeling that I wasn't going to make the street. I had no fear. Death was better than living through the shit I was facing. If I got out alive, I'd do the same crap over and over.

Softball was what kept me alive. I was playing with the old-timers' team. I played second base, and Andy played in the outfield. I was great with the bullshit. I would insult the guy who was up at bat with the most outlandish crap. No one was safe from the onslaught of words to demean the person. When we played the blacks, I would rip into them. I had the blacks in the bleachers laughing their asses off. With the Spanish team, I was able to talk and use gestures. It was a lot of fun.

When the playoffs came around, things got heated up. If something was going down, I would jump right in to the fray and break it up. The screws let me do their work. Most of the time the guys were face to face or nose to nose. The thing was, everyone was having a good time.

I was coming up on seven years served, and I was to see the parole board for the first time. I had to see a woman who took the information she needed to give to the parole board. As she interviewed me, she wanted to know about a number of crimes I had committed. She told me that it was refreshing to read something other than a crime that was committed by a person armed with a bag of rocks. She asked me about the time that I was a fugitive and wanted to know how I supported.

I told her about the boat yard and said that I did not commit any crimes. She said, "That's because you never got caught."

I responded very quickly, "What did you want me to do, run for mayor?"

She let out a scream, buried her face in her hands, and was sobbing with laughter. I entered the parole office. They were looking me over and asked me if I had any remorse for what I had done with my life. I decided to tell the truth. On the day I entered Walpole, I was confronted with an insane asylum and had to live a life of fear and nightmares with animals I had a profound hatred for. I made an oath that my life as a criminal was over. I had not changed a bit, but I knew it was not the life for me. Walpole was my savior; it was my Christ. I then told the parole board, "If you deny me parole, it would not bother me in the least. I know who I am now and what is in store for me!"

They asked a lot of stupid questions. They wanted to know how many banks I had robbed. I told them that I had lost count. They told me to step out of the room. I was out about five minutes when they called me into the room and told me that I was denied parole. The spokesman said that I had to go to prerelease and work for a year, and then he said, "You should sell your story."

I applied for prerelease and had to take a drug test. I took the test and was told that I had drugs in my blood. I was placed in a strip cell for fourteen days. Everyone in the institution knew I was the last guy who would ever take a drug. A female screw came to interview me about the drug in my system. I told her, "There is a drug in my system. The drug analyzer doesn't lie. Someone who dispenses the drugs gave it to me mistakenly or deliberately. I know someone wants me to be denied to go to prerelease."

I told the correctional officer that every guy in the institution knew that I preached against drugs. I said to the correctional officer, "Whatever you do to me is nothing. I can take what you dish out. The one who is going to lose is the institution; the institution will lose all credibility."

Two weeks later I was sent to prerelease. I was told that the parole board set a date to see me. I sent a form letter that I wanted to complete my sentence and be set free. Prerelease was okay. I got a job in a recycling plant. I was up to the challenge. I stood in one position all day long and separated plastic from cans. I got into a routine and produced a huge amount of work. The manager took me aside and said that the production was way up and when I got out, I had a job if I wanted it.

I had less than one year left on my sentence. Some inmate walked off and was involved in a shooting of a police officer. On that very day, anyone who was involved in a violent crime was sent back to Norfolk Penitentiary. I had one more year to go, and that was the longest year in my life. I plunged into schooling. Every free moment I had, I would study math and vocabulary. The words fascinated me. It seemed to cure me. I was thinking better and sleeping better. I looked at things in a different light. I completely understood that people forgive, but they cannot forget. I found out that once people know the extent of your criminality, they find it impossible to be around you for any length of time. I had to find a way to live my life and be happy without infringing on the lives of others.

This book is not going to help me in the least; it's only going to provoke people. My family is already provoked. I don't want to be invisible! My only hope is to be successful and become a celebrity. My only fear is that it's hard to differentiate between a celebrity and a clown.

I never tried to make a person who detested me into a friend. I checked people out. If someone did not respond to me, I said nothing more and moved on. Now that I am much older, I need very little. The struggle is over. I'm content to view sex voyeuristically. My time is coming to an end. My partner in crime, Henry Caron, died three months after I escaped. Ron was killed by rifle fire. Claude was killed by a gunshot. Anthony was killed with two others. Tommy Desimone was killed. *Jimmy Burke* died a natural death. Since I'm not using full names, I'll just say that countless others were murdered, maimed, and tortured!